ACCLAIM FOR *SISTER EVE, PRIVATE EYE*

"Lynne Hinton grabs you and doesn't let go until the last page is turned. I hope, no, I pray we haven't heard the last from Sister Eve, private eye."

—PHIL GULLEY, BESTSELLING
AUTHOR OF THE HARMONY SERIES

"Lynne Hinton has created a marvelous character in Sister Eve Divine. This nun-turned-detective will keep an enduring hold on your heart and mind long after the case is solved and the roar of her Harley fades into the desert air."

—MARK DE CASTRIQUE, *A
MURDER IN PASSING*

"Lynne Hinton's reverently irreverent Sister Eve is my new hero. This is not just a well-crafted, page-turning mystery—this is a grounded, believable and enlightened examination of family dynamics, internal emotional and spiritual struggles and the choices human beings make. The characters are complex and multi-dimensional—readers will find themselves relating to them with ease. An absolute joy to read."

—MAGGI PETTON, AUTHOR OF
THE QUEEN'S COMPANION AND
HEAVEN'S DAUGHTER

"In *Sister Eve, Private Eye*, Lynne Hinton has once again created a central character who is fascinating, flawed, funny, and compellingly human: Sister Evangeline Divine, the Harley-riding Benedictine nun . . . With her signature combination of warm, folksy characters and down-home style, Hinton strikes just the right note with *Sister Eve*—a blend of humor, suspense, wit, and incisive flashes of philosophical insight. *Sister Eve* is a winner."

—PENELOPE J. STOKES, AUTHOR OF
*THE BLUE BOTTLE CLUB, CIRCLE OF
GRACE* AND *SAINT SOMEDAY*

"Although *Sister Eve, Private Eye* is laced with humor, this eponymous nun neatly sidesteps the potential pitfalls of cuteness. Lynne Hinton writes with grace and compassion and I look forward to learning where she'll take Sister Eve next."

—MARGARET MARON, EDGAR
AWARD-WINNING AUTHOR OF *THE
BOOTLEGGER'S DAUGHTER*

"With keen insight into the life of one who has used her life's calling for God, Hinton paints a complex and realistic heroine who is sure to win the hearts of readers. Fans of *The Mitford* series and *Murder She Wrote* are certain to soak up every page of this well written and delightful novel. I can't wait to read Sister Eve's next adventure in this series."

—MICHAEL MORRIS, AUTHOR OF
MAN IN THE BLUE MOON

ACCLAIM FOR *THE ART OF ARRANGING FLOWERS*

"Will leave you with a contented sigh and a hopeful heart."

—*NEW YORK TIMES* BESTSELLING
AUTHOR KAREN WHITE

"I devoured this book. There is art and beauty in this story that will linger after the final scene."

—DEBBIE MACOMBER, #1 *NEW
YORK TIMES* BESTSELLING AUTHOR
OF *ROSE HARBOR IN BLOOM* AND
STARRY NIGHT

"An expertly penned and tender tale about the blossoming of hearts amidst the storms of loss and grief."

—RICHARD PAUL EVANS, #1 *NEW
YORK TIMES* AND *USA TODAY*
BESTSELLING AUTHOR

SISTER EVE,
PRIVATE EYE

LYNNE HINTON

THOMAS NELSON
Since 1798

NASHVILLE   MEXICO CITY   RIO DE JANEIRO

Published in Nashville, Tennessee, by Thomas Nelson. Thomas Nelson is a registered trademark of HarperCollins Christian Publishing, Inc.

Thomas Nelson titles may be purchased in bulk for educational, business, fund-raising, or sales promotional use. For information, please email SpecialMarkets@ ThomasNelson.com.

Publisher's Note: This novel is a work of fiction. Names, characters, places, and incidents are either products of the author's imagination or used fictitiously. All characters are fictional, and any similarity to people living or dead is purely coincidental.

Library of Congress Cataloging-in-Publication Data

Hinton, J. Lynne.
  Sister Eve, private eye / Lynne Hinton.
    pages cm. -- (A Divine Private Detective Agency mystery ; 1)
  ISBN 978-1-4016-9145-5 (paperback)
1. Nuns--Fiction. 2. Private investigators--Fiction. I. Title.
  PS3558.I457S57 2014
  813'.54--dc23

                              2014023477

Printed in the United States of America

14 15 16 17 18 19 RRD 6 5 4 3 2 1

PROLOGUE

Chaz Cheston grabbed his keys and quietly made his way out the back door. He had exactly one hour and fifteen minutes to pick up the final pages of the script and drive to the airport in Santa Fe. A jet was arriving that morning to pick him up and make a quick turnaround trip back to California. He stood beside his prized sports car, patted the bulging pocket of his black leather jacket, and glanced at his watch. He was late.

Ron Polland had arranged back-to-back meetings in Los Angeles that morning. Cheston was scheduled to check in with the assistant director at ten o'clock, the casting director at ten thirty, and the director of photography at eleven. Polland, the producer, was expecting the director at the studio production offices at noon. There was a lunch planned for the investors later, and the entire afternoon was to be devoted to the final budget approval. Cheston just hoped that Polland wouldn't ask for a statement from the production account at the bank before the meetings. He jumped in the car, turned on the engine, and sped down the driveway.

Cheston planned to take the meetings, hand over the finished pages, and get his check so he could make the deposit before the withdrawal had been noticed. The assistant manager at the bank, the tall blonde taking evening acting classes, had already given him a heads-up that Polland had asked for weekly statements for the account. Chaz thought about the woman, recalling how he had arranged a personal studio tour and suggested that she would be great in his next project, a lie he would deal with later.

He knew that Polland was already suspicious about what had happened to the advance. Just out of rehab, Chaz wouldn't even be hired by the studio without insurance. He couldn't shake that monkey off his back no matter how hard he tried. Polland had not been happy when his star writer and director had flown to New Mexico more than a month ago claiming he needed to be on location to finish the script for the film he'd promised would start production in three weeks.

It was just before dawn, and the sun was still well below the barren peaks of the Ortiz Mountains marking the horizon to the east. The temperature was cooler than he'd expected, and he turned up the heat. He headed down the winding dirt road that would curve and dip for a couple of miles before hitting Highway 14. He recalled that the main drag through Madrid and Cerrillos was known as the Turquoise Trail, a forty-mile stretch of desert highway between Albuquerque and Santa Fe.

He switched his headlights to bright, taking the curves as fast as he could. He recalled the directions he had used a few times before, trying to remember the exact route number and cattle guards to count. It was at least a thirty-minute drive to the cabin outside of Madrid and then at least forty-five more to the airport. But all he had to do was drive by, pick up the necessary pages, drop off some cash, and he'd soon be on his way to Santa Fe. He'd figure out the other details of explaining his whereabouts later.

Chaz cursed. If Ross had just e-mailed the pages to him, it would have saved him a needless, time-consuming trip. But he'd refused. He was sticking to his usual writing tool of an IBM Selectric typewriter, and if Chaz wanted this story by Ross Biltmore, he was going to get it the way Ross Biltmore wrote them all: single-spaced narrative style, half-inch margins, Times Roman font, size 12. Somebody else was going to have to indent the pages of dialogue, add the characters' names to the lines, and supply the scene directions. He didn't care if there was a close-up on the hero or if the location was an interior or exterior, Ross Biltmore just wrote the story.

Chaz Cheston headed east toward the rising sun, the sports car throwing up pebbles and raising dust in swirls behind him. Chaz and Ross had known each other since college, rooming together the last couple of years of school, although that didn't really mean anything since Chaz was never there. By the time Ross left the university and traveled across India to study with some religious guru, Chaz, son of a famous movie director and grandson of a well-respected producer, was already working as an assistant to an assistant director in a major Hollywood production.

In the beginning, Ross simply wrote term papers and essays for Chaz, but then he began taking his roommate's exams when he could. However, in twenty years that arrangement had evolved. Ross withdrew from his classes the second semester of his junior year but remained a resident in the luxury apartment near campus paid for by the Cheston family. He turned out to be a gifted writer. No one at the university ever found out about the forged papers, and no one in the industry knew where Chaz Cheston came up with his brilliant ideas for movies.

Only Chaz and Ross knew the man who was really the genius behind the romantic comedies and the action-packed dramas. And for twenty years, that's the way it had been for the two friends. As far as Chaz knew, Ross never minded the anonymity, the lack of recognition, and he never asked for more money than what was offered. It was a solid business arrangement, and Chaz couldn't be happier. Especially now.

He made the turn on 14 and headed north. The sun was just starting to peek over the top of the Sangre de Cristos. He made the second left onto the dirt road and hit the accelerator. From this point it was a straight shot to the house near Cedar Hill. He was still hoping to make good time.

When he arrived at the entry to Ross's property, the fourth cattle guard and the second driveway off the road, he put the car in park and got out. He walked up to the gate, reached around, and slid the gate lock open, as he had been taught by Ross, and grabbed the small key he had been given from the pocket of his jacket. He opened the lock on the chain that was wrapped around the fence and the gate, yanked it through, pushed the gate, jumped back in his car, and pulled in, leaving the gate open. He hurried toward the small cabin built on the north side of a mesa. Stopping at the end of the drive, Chaz turned off the engine and waited. He looked around the house to see if any lights were on and then got out of the car, heading to the back door.

Why on earth would anyone want to live way out here? he asked himself and shook his head as he searched around him, making sure no one else was there. Feeling confident that he was alone, he walked to the porch and searched for the folder he'd been promised.

Ross had explained when Chaz called over the weekend that he was heading out of town but that he had finished the script, and the final scenes would be left under a blanket on a rocking chair on the east side of the house. He asked that Chaz put the cash and the gate key in the SentrySafe at the other end of the property. Chaz had been given the combination, and after picking up the script, he planned to drive down to the barn and drop off the bundle of cash he had zipped in his jacket pocket.

Ross, he had been instructed a long time ago, never wanted a check or direct deposit. He wanted cash only. No paper trail was just fine with the Hollywood filmmaker.

Chaz eyed the outdoor furniture lining the long porch. There were two rocking chairs near the front door and another near a bench. Sure enough, the thick folder was under the old red Navajo blanket. Relieved, he stuck the folder under his arm and was heading to his car when he saw the lights coming up the driveway.

It was still not quite sunrise, and the small, round beams of light bounced up and down as they moved closer and closer to him. Chaz stood, frozen, watching as the vehicle pulled up beside his. The driver's door opened. At first he thought it must be Ross home early, or maybe a neighbor, someone who watched the property when the owner was gone. He was squinting, trying to see who was getting out of the car, when he heard his name called and recognized the voice before he ever saw the face.

"Christ, have mercy . . ." He felt a sharp pain in the left part of his chest and the folder under his arm fall. He dropped to his knees, the papers flying all around him, looking down at where he had been shot. He reached for his chest, expecting to find blood, but soon realized that what was lodged firmly under his skin was not a bullet but a short, thin dart. He looked up.

"I always heard the desert was a spiritual place, Charles." The familiar face loomed over him. He felt tightness in his chest and pain radiating across his shoulders and down his left arm. The Hollywood director struggled for breath. "I just never figured you for the religious type," were the last words Chaz Cheston ever heard.

ONE

"Pssst . . ." The sound was a faint whisper and came from the chapel entrance.

Sister Evangeline heard the noise but did not rise from her kneeling position; instead, she simply redoubled her prayers for patience. Breakfast had been served and it was an hour past Lauds. After a quick ride to the town of Glorieta to clear her head, she had returned to the sanctuary for an extended period of scripture reading and meditation meant to aid her spiritual journey. She heard the whisper but remained at the kneeling bench, the narrow beam hard beneath her knees. Candles burned on the altar, and the statue of Mary stood above the nun as she prayed. Saints watched from the stained-glass windows as she closed her eyes and took in a breath. Maybe the whisper was not meant for her, she decided.

She readjusted herself, folded her hands once again, and bowed lower. The pew she was on was empty except for her helmet, which had been placed beside her. Even though she hadn't actually worn it during the ride, she took it with her just to keep the questions and criticisms at bay. She couldn't help herself—she snuck a peek at it just to make sure it was still there. Satisfied that it had not been taken, she drew in a deep breath and began a recitation from the Psalms.

She wanted to be obedient. She tried to be dutiful, and if being able to accomplish such a feat required extra prayers, Sister Evangeline was willing to do it. Lately the well-seasoned nun had confessed to experiencing difficulty remaining patient with other members of her order at Our Lady of Guadalupe Abbey and with some of the changes being made at the direction of the Santa Fe diocese, especially the new order that was requiring the nuns to move out. She and Brother Oliver, the vice superior of the monastery that historically housed both monks and nuns, had agreed that additional time of solitude and prayers might aid her with her personal weaknesses, especially her anger. He had meant clocking hours in the chapel, but Evangeline knew that a ride on her Harley calmed and centered her more than sitting in a quiet room. So she decided to do them both. She finished the recitation and began her prayer.

"Pssst . . ."

There it was again. She remained bowed. She kept her eyes closed. *Maybe someone else was in the chapel, maybe someone was sitting behind her and was being called*, she thought. Maybe they would take the cue of her silence and leave quietly. Or maybe whoever was trying to capture her attention would realize Evangeline was in prayer and leave her alone.

"Psssst . . . pssst . . . pssst."

She rose up and jerked her head around. "What?!" she barked.

Clearly Brother Oliver had been right; she needed divine assistance.

Evangeline shook her head. "I'm sorry," she said as gently as she could to the young novice standing at the door, her pale face peeking through the opening. "Sister Margaret, please, come in, come in." She sat up from the kneeling bench to the pew and waved the young woman inside. She rested her elbows on her knees.

"Sister Divine . . ."

"It's *Diveen*. It's pronounced *Diveen*, not Divine. And just call me Sister Eve or Sister Evangeline; you don't call us by our last names."

"I'm so sorry. I'm sorry." The novice had been at the monastery only a couple of weeks and was still learning the names of the sisters and the proper ways to address them. She was thin and nervous, and she stood just inside the chapel entrance, her voice so low Evangeline could hardly hear her.

Evangeline blew out a long breath. "It's fine."

There was a long pause as Evangeline waited. Finally she raised her hands, a clear question being asked.

"Oh, right . . ." The young woman cleared her throat, remembering her reason for interrupting her elder. "There's someone here to see you." She didn't move any closer.

Likely a guest wanting to talk about the meal schedule or the linens in the room. In her role as manager of Guest Services at the monastery, she handled all the special requests and complaints from those who used the facilities for private retreats or group meetings. Talking over her shoulder, she said, "Take down their name and room number, and I will be with them in an hour." Eve turned and bowed her head once again.

The young nun stood at the door, shifting her weight from side to side, trying to decide what to do. She was breathing fairly loudly.

Sister Evangeline could tell the novice had not left. "Is there anything else?" she asked, without looking up and trying not to sound impatient.

Margaret kept her head down. "It's a policeman, Sister. He said it was an emergency."

"Well, why didn't you say so to begin with?" She stood up, leaving the helmet, and walked to the end of the pew, genuflected, crossed herself, and headed toward the door. "Margaret, you have got to learn to be more assertive about these kinds of things."

"Yes, Sister," she said as the older nun hurried past her.

The police officer stood on the porch outside the main entrance of the monastery. He was tall and wore a dark suit with a badge clipped onto his right front pocket. An investigator, perhaps? He was watching a group of nuns walking down to the river. She opened the door and stepped out, allowing the door to slam hard behind her. The officer, startled, placed his hands securely on the weapons attached to his belt. Sister Eve stood at the door, the hem of her long, gray habit caught in the top of her cowboy boots.

She studied the man, folded her arms across her chest, and said, "I will not talk to you without an attorney present."

TWO

"Well, if you aren't going to talk, then I guess I'll just have to arrest you and take you downtown," the officer replied, maintaining his stance.

There was a pause and then big smiles from them both.

"Daniel," Eve responded, hurrying in his direction and giving him a big hug. "It is so good to see you!" She pulled away and looked up at her father's oldest friend and former partner.

"Did you finally see the error of your ways and come to make your confession?" She punched the man in the arm. "I hope you packed to stay overnight."

He was still grinning. "Ah, little Sister, maybe I'm here because of all those speeding tickets you seem to forget to pay."

She rolled her eyes. "There has only been one speeding ticket in this calendar year, and I know for a fact the monastery paid it."

"Oh, so now who has to spend all day in confession?" He grinned. "And it's still early in the year."

She laughed.

"You still got your pets?" he asked, looking around.

"Not so many," she answered. "They told me I could only keep four." She signaled to the building behind her, inferring the powers that be at the convent. "They claim I'm trying to turn the monastery into an animal shelter."

"Well, are you?" he asked.

She shrugged. "Maybe."

"They still going to make you move?" The news had been in the local papers. Everyone knew about the changes being called for at the monastery. Eve had been quoted in the stories and had gotten into trouble for speaking to the press.

She only nodded.

"You go out riding?"

She smiled.

"You wear your helmet?" He looked in the direction of where her bike was parked.

She cleared her throat and turned away, remembering that she had left her helmet on the pew in the chapel. "The sisters bought me a new one," she answered. "They gave it to me at Christmas."

An old dog walked up and she bent down to greet it.

"That's not what I asked."

She could feel his stare. She stood up and the dog sat at her feet. "Last I heard, New Mexico doesn't require helmets." She dusted off her hands on the front of her habit.

"Just because there's no law against riding without a helmet doesn't mean you shouldn't use common sense. God don't honor foolishness."

Eve laughed. "You're starting to sound like him," she said.

"He's right about some things." He glanced around the monastery. "They get the new building started?"

She looked over at the planned building site for the new living quarters. The fact that the women were being kicked out and not able to have a say in where they went was only part of the reason she was angry about the changes. She thought separating the monks from the nuns and building new housing was ridiculous. She also thought it made more sense to build a kennel for the stray animals than a new housing area for the nuns. It wasn't like they said—she didn't want to change the monastery into an animal shelter, but she had been pushing for a facility for stray animals for years. With the new changes pushing the nuns out, she had finally been told to leave the matter of a kennel alone. She shook away the thoughts.

"Still working on it," she answered. She turned back to the officer. "Where are my manners? Won't you come in for a cup of tea?" She took him by the arm, leading him to the steps.

He stopped her. "Actually, this isn't exactly a social call, Evangeline. I came because I need to talk to you about something."

She dropped his arm and turned to him.

He looked back to the car he was driving. There was someone sitting in the backseat.

"It's the Captain," he responded. "Your dad," he added, even though he was sure Eve knew who the Captain was.

Evangeline looked back at the officer, forgetting about his passenger.

"He's at the hospital. He has to have surgery."

"What kind of surgery?" Eve asked. She slid a piece of hair underneath the white veil she wore covering her head.

"It's his leg," Daniel replied. "They have to amputate it."

"Amputate it? I just talked to him last week, and he said the toe was getting better."

Captain Jackson Divine had been a brittle diabetic for a long time, but in the last year he had battled infections in his lower extremities, including the most recent one involving his big toe.

Daniel shook his head. "After four rounds of antibiotics, it didn't go away. The infection was spreading faster than they could manage. The doctors told him there was no other choice. It has to come off." He waited. "The foot and part of the leg."

Eve made the sign of the cross and closed her eyes. She couldn't believe what she was hearing. "I never thought it would progress this quickly," she noted and paused. "Wait, how long have you known the infection was this bad?"

Daniel cleared his throat, uncomfortable with the question. He had been friends with Captain Divine for more than thirty years. He had watched Eve and her sister, Dorisanne, grow up. He was aware that the man had ongoing issues of privacy and pride. He shook his head. This was not easy news for him to report.

Eve could see his discomfort and waved off the question. "Never mind, it doesn't matter. It's not your fault that he doesn't tell me anything. This is just like him, waiting until the last minute and then making you drive out here to break the news."

A car pulled up and parked in the lot next to the front entrance. The two of them turned and watched as a couple got out and headed in the direction of the chapel. Eve assumed they had an appointment with one of the monks. She had heard about a couple who were planning to have their wedding held in the chapel later in the spring.

"I came to take you to the hospital," Daniel explained. "The surgery is this afternoon."

"This afternoon? Today?" Eve sighed. "Did you call Dorisanne?"

He shook his head. "I don't have her new number."

Eve nodded. She wasn't even sure she had a correct number to reach her little sister. Dorisanne was known to change residences and contact information on a fairly regular basis.

"She's still in Vegas. I'll try the number I have before we leave." She looked again over at her bike parked near the main building. She reached out, squeezing the man on the arm. "Daniel, it was really nice of you to come and tell me the news, but I need to take care of a few things before I go. I'd rather drive myself to St. Vincent's," she said, knowing that she needed to talk to her superiors about her situation.

"I'd feel better if I drove you," Daniel responded. "I have some phone calls to make, so don't hurry. I'll just wait in the car until you're ready."

And that's when Evangeline finally remembered the person she had seen in the backseat of Daniel's car. She peered over in that direction.

"You stop on the way and make an arrest?" she asked, trying to get a better view.

It appeared to be a woman, but Eve wasn't sure. All she could see was a large, dark hat. Either the person was small or was sitting slumped in the seat. Her face was down, and the hat kept Eve from getting a good look.

Daniel glanced at the car. "Oh, no, she's not a perp. She's your father's client."

Eve was confused. "His client? Well, who is it?"

Daniel fidgeted, shifting his weight from side to side.

"Are you blushing?" Eve asked. "You are! But why? Who is it?" she asked again and strained to get a better look.

Daniel cleared his throat. "The Captain was working on a missing person's case when the doctor gave him the news." He motioned in the direction of the car. "She was with him in the emergency room when he called me. When I got there, she asked to come with me to tell you."

Eve shielded her eyes from the late-morning sun. Suddenly, as if the unknown passenger had been beckoned, the door opened and out stepped a pair of slender, tan legs, bearing the weight of the most glamorous young woman the nun had ever seen. There was a perfect smile radiating from the perfect face beneath the large, fashionable hat.

"You must be Sister Evangeline," the woman said as she walked up to Eve and stuck out her small, well-manicured hand. Eve looked over at Daniel, who dropped his eyes and backed away.

"I have heard everything about you. I am Megan Flint. Your father is—how shall I put this?" She glanced at Daniel. "He's very dear to me."

THREE

―――――・❦❦❦・―――――

"I'm sorry," Eve responded, not offering her hand. "Do we know each other?" She looked at the young woman and then at Daniel, who was not answering.

"I'm Megan Flint," she repeated, saying the name as if she thought the nun should recognize it.

Eve gave no response.

The lack of recognition seemed to come as a surprise. She shook her head as if to say never mind. "Your father was trying to find my fiancé," she noted, stepping back a bit, giving Eve a little more room. "He's been missing a week, and I'm sick with worry."

Eve watched the young woman. "Are you from Santa Fe?"

"Los Angeles," she answered. "And my fiancé has been in Madrid. That's how I met your father."

Eve nodded. "And you were with him in the emergency room at the hospital because . . . ?"

"Oh, I had my driver take Captain Divine to the hospital once

17

the nurse at the clinic in Cerrillos informed us he needed to go right away."

Eve still didn't respond. She was trying to put the facts together.

Daniel moved forward to help fill in the blanks. "Megan hired the Captain when her boyfriend didn't show up in Los Angeles last week. His name is Charles Cheston." He waited as if Eve would recognize that name. When she didn't, he continued, "He's a famous movie director." He paused. "*The Sound of a Trombone*? *Saved from Drowning*?"

Eve thought these were the names of movies but she wasn't sure, so she shrugged.

"You never saw *The Sound of a Trombone*?" Daniel sounded very surprised.

"I'm a nun, Daniel. We don't have a lot of time for the cinema."

"Yeah, but you used to love movies," he noted. He looked at the entrance of the monastery. "You can't go to a movie?" he asked.

Eve rolled her eyes. "Why were you with him at the clinic?" she asked the young woman again.

Megan seemed confused. "Chaz wasn't at the clinic." She stopped. "He's not sick."

Eve turned to Daniel, hoping he could help out his passenger.

"Oh, you mean your father!" The young woman finally seemed to catch on.

"I had an appointment with him at his office this morning. We were to go over his recent findings. There's a man in Madrid who apparently knows Chaz. Your father thought he might have some answers about his whereabouts. Anyway, when I arrived, Jack was coming out the door and said he needed to go to the clinic.

He seemed a little unsteady so I told him that Matthew, that's my driver, would take him and that we could just have our meeting on the drive over and back." She glanced at Daniel, explaining, "I thought it was just a checkup or something."

Eve nodded.

"But after the nurse examined him, she informed him that he had to go to the hospital. She wanted to call an ambulance, but I told her I would drive him to Santa Fe." She shrugged. "So that's what I did."

"Matthew did," Eve responded.

"What?"

"Matthew drove him to Santa Fe," Eve corrected her.

"Yes, right. I don't drive, so yes, Matthew drove us to the hospital."

"And then the Captain called you?" Eve asked Daniel.

Daniel nodded.

"I don't know what I would do without your father," the young woman said with a note of sadness in her voice. Her face reddened. "Not that I think anything is going to happen to him," she added, backpedaling. "Oh my, I didn't mean to sound like I think he's going to die or something. Please forgive me, Sister." She appeared flustered. "I'm not saying anything right." She shook her head, the big hat nearly hitting Eve in the face.

"It's fine," Eve said. "Let me just get some things taken care of, and I'll be ready to go." She turned to Daniel. "You want to bring Ms. Flint in to wait?"

"Oh, I would love to come into your convent." Megan moved past Eve and the dog at her feet and headed for the front steps. "I auditioned last year for a role as a nun in an HBO special." She was already at the front door. "Turns out they went with an actress they said looked more like a nun, you know, one whose looks were a little less . . ." She stopped and smiled at Eve. "They went with another actress," she restated. "I was really disappointed because I've always been fascinated with nuns. I thought if I got the part I could meet Mother Teresa and learn about nuns from her. Do you pray all the time?" She waited only a second and continued, "Anyway, instead, I ended up getting the role in Chaz's gangster movie. I played a prostitute. I never really did much research for that part." She laughed at her own joke, then stood smiling at the door.

"Mother Teresa is dead," Eve pointed out.

"Oh, how sad," Megan replied sincerely. She paused. "I guess it was good I didn't get the part then."

And before Evangeline and Daniel could even respond, the young woman had walked in through the front doors. Eve turned to the officer.

"She's an actress," he explained.

"She's something," Eve replied. And she left him standing at his car and followed the young woman inside.

FOUR

Aaron Valdez was not a native of Madrid, New Mexico, but he knew the terrain as if he had lived there all his life. He was actually from Las Cruces, southern territory, but when he was just a boy, he was shipped off to live with an aunt and uncle after his parents divorced and neither one of them wanted him. He was a shy young man who had more to do with the horses at the Silver Cross Corral than he did with the tourists who came for trail rides or the locals who loved to gossip and share tales.

John Ewing was the owner of the ranch and trail-ride establishment. He came up from Abilene, Texas, in the early sixties, made a killing in the silver mines, and bought up as much of the land near Cerrillos and the old Turquoise Trail as he could afford and that wasn't already owned by the state of New Mexico. Later he brought in a bunch of horses and set up the stables. He opened up the Silver Cross for trail rides in the late eighties on the property bordering the Cerrillos Hills State Park. He didn't make a lot of money taking tourists out in the wilderness, but everyone who knew John understood he didn't do it to make money; he had all that he needed. He did it because he loved the land, and he wanted anyone who would make the drive from Santa Fe or Albuquerque over to the little towns of Madrid and Cerrillos to love it too.

Aaron was his only full-time employee. The rancher hired one or two others during the business high seasons, late spring, summer, and early fall, but they were usually just a couple of kids who would saddle and feed the horses while he and Aaron handled the rides. The two men had been together for ten years, and both of them considered themselves quite lucky to have the arrangement they had made. The folks in Madrid laughed that John Ewing and Aaron Valdez were closer than any married couple in town. The only difference, they would tease the rancher and the cowboy, was that the two men never fussed or kissed. John and Aaron secretly understood, however, that only half of that statement was true.

They never discussed the one moment of intimacy. They never talked about the awkward way the older man leaned in to his employee late on a Friday night after a busload of college students finished a day of riding, the way he smelled of hay and whiskey. There had never been a conversation to explain why John did what he did and how it felt to Aaron, who had quickly jumped up and walked away after the kiss. There had been no discussion between the two about the event, and there had been no more advances between the rancher and his hired hand.

It was late in the month of February, the twenty-second to be exact, when John asked Aaron to take a couple staying in Santa Fe down to Galisteo Creek and over to the dam out along the railroad tracks. Aaron thought it was odd that his boss had asked him to handle the two riders, since he knew that having the chance to talk to a small number of people was what John loved most. With just one or two visitors, the rancher was able to have a real conversation and not have to yell so often to make sure that the line of people behind him could hear. And with fewer riders, John could travel farther and have a greater chance to ride his horse the way he liked, with more gallop than saunter.

Still, it wasn't completely unheard of for Aaron to be asked to manage the trail rides. He saddled up Molly and Lucy, two of the older mares, since he wasn't sure of the two guests' levels of riding experience. Molly and Lucy were gentle and harmless; neither of them had ever bucked or kicked. Whether the guests were beginners or experienced, Aaron knew he couldn't go wrong with the two easy rides.

"Just take them out to the dam," John had said as he got into his truck to leave. "And make sure you charge the full amount; that coupon in the magazines expired at the end of the year. That two-for-one special was a stupid move on my part!" And with that, a wave of his hand, and an affectionate nod, he started the engine and left. He didn't tell Aaron where he was heading.

Aaron was happy to spend his morning on a ride. Snow from the week before still covered the ground. He thought the hills were most beautiful in the winter and was looking forward to heading out past the old mines and up to the dam. It was one of his favorite trail rides.

The couple arrived right on time, and as soon as they stepped out of their SUV, both of them wearing new cowboy boots and designer jeans, Aaron was glad he had saddled the two old horses. He could spot city slickers a mile away.

"For heaven's sake, William, why did you have to pick a place so far out?" The woman stumbled over a rock and was quickly steadied by her companion walking beside her.

"It's supposed to have great views," he explained, still holding her arm. "I saw it on the Internet, and the concierge said this was the best."

Aaron heard the woman mumble something under her breath, and suddenly he wasn't as enthusiastic about the morning ride as he had been earlier. It was easy to see that this would be more babysitting than trail riding.

They made their introductions and after collecting their money, Aaron helped them both onto their horses. The woman was notice-ably frightened. She began pulling the reins too tightly, causing Molly to struggle against her. Aaron tried to explain that while rid-ing she didn't have to yank so hard, that the horse knew the trail and could be trusted, but it didn't matter. The woman squeezed her legs together and held on for dear life even while they were still standing at the stables. The man, Aaron noted, did not fare much better. He kept shifting from side to side so violently Lucy was beginning to act skittish, something the old mare never did.

Aaron mounted his horse, Clover, deciding against the long ride to the dam and choosing instead to lead them on the short trail just up from the ranch to the top of the Cerrillos Hills, out past the old cemetery, and back down on the south side, home by way of the San Marcos wash. The trail was narrow in parts but not dangerous, and once at the top, the scenery always made for a good photo opportunity. Even though the trip was only a few miles long and would take them less than the reserved hour and a half, he would gladly refund their deposit if they weren't happy. By the way the two were handling their horses, Aaron knew he did not want to extend this ride any longer than he had to.

They had just made the final switchback and were standing at the top of the hill where the views were long and clear. The woman's horse, Molly, had stopped, and with Aaron's direction had turned to face the east, offering her rider the vista of blue horizon and the scrub-brush desert floor, still white from the week of snow. Lucy had walked the man over to a small clump of bear grass and was trying to get a bite, and even though Aaron normally would have stopped the horse from grazing, he chose to let the horse do as she wished while he turned toward the south, trying to make out Las Lomas de la Bolsa.

The woman's scream was so loud and unexpected, Aaron jumped. He pulled on Clover's reins, and the big horse began backing up, plowing right into Lucy, which caused her to buck and drop the male customer off to the side.

"Whoa! Whoa!" Aaron called out, finally able to grab Lucy's reins, jump off Clover, take control of both horses, and make sure the man wasn't hurt. It was a few minutes before he was able to attend to the woman and discover the reason for her scream.

"Jessica, what on earth is wrong with you!" the man yelled as he stood, dusting himself off. "I could have broken my neck!"

"There!" she screamed. "Look, down there!" And she pointed below them to the Gallina Arroyo where some of the snow had melted.

Still holding the reins of both horses and able to assess that the man was not seriously hurt, Aaron could see that the woman had not pulled or yanked her horse and that Molly appeared calm even as the other two horses remained spooked. He followed the woman's outstretched arm, the point of her finger, and could barely make out what was lying in the wash. A torso and two legs could be seen where the snow was just starting to melt.

"It's a body," the woman said softly and then fainted, falling backward, letting go of the reins, and dropping to the ground right into a fresh pile of Molly's manure.

FIVE

"Why are you driving so slow?" Evangeline was in the front seat with Daniel and had closed the car door on the hem of her habit. She yanked and pulled as Megan Flint watched from her seat in the back.

"I am driving the speed limit," Daniel said. "Put your seat belt on." He turned and noticed Eve as she struggled with her clothes. "What is wrong with you?"

Eve blew out a long breath and buckled herself in. "I'm caught in the door. I hate these stupid, long things." She pulled once more, finally freeing herself. "At least I can still wear the boots." She smiled as Daniel looked down at her cowboy boots.

He shook his head. "I thought the mother in charge told you not to wear those."

"She's mother superior, and she told me I could wear them when I ride. I was out this morning and didn't have a chance to change into the sensible nun shoes."

"You wear your habit on the bike?"

She shook her head and pulled up the bottom of the garment. Jeans were stuffed into her boots. "I'll take this off when we get there."

"I don't know, maybe dressed like a nun you'll get better treatment at the hospital." Daniel grinned.

"The habit is not meant to garner better treatment," she replied.

Megan piped up from the backseat. "Right, a habit reveals that the nuns are women who have dedicated themselves to a life of prayer, sacrifice, and penance. The habit is a visible manifestation for people to know and see that nuns are giving their lives for others, for the salvation of the world, and for God's glory."

Eve turned around in her seat. "You learned all that for the part in a movie?"

Megan looked up. "No, I just googled it."

Eve stared at her for a minute and then turned back to face the front. She decided not to comment further about the habit or the movie star's answer. She cleared her throat. "You know, he always said you drove like an old woman."

Daniel gripped the steering wheel. "Because he has the same problem with a heavy foot that you have." When he realized what he had said and the irony of it, he shook his head. "Sorry."

"Don't be sorry. We both know that even a plastic foot isn't going to slow him down," she responded.

There was a pause.

"I'm taking care of Trooper," Daniel said. "I'll pick her up tonight."

Eve nodded. "Thanks," she said. "I know that means a lot to him. We all know he loves dogs better than he loves people."

"I would say that's something else the two of you have in common." He reached over and gently elbowed Eve in the side.

She didn't respond because as much as she didn't want to admit it, the statement was closer to the truth than not. She did love animals and believed that they were easier to get along with than people.

They drove along in silence, and then Eve turned around in her seat. "Why didn't you call the police about your missing boyfriend?"

Megan looked up, surprised that she was being spoken to. She was still doing something on her cell phone, looking up other interesting details on the Internet, Eve figured, or maybe texting. She had seen some of the visitors at the monastery typing on their phones. They had explained the unfamiliar mode of communication to her when she asked about it. In the end, she thought it seemed like a waste of time.

"Oh, I did," she answered. "They claimed he hadn't been missing long enough to file a report."

"Earlier you called him your fiancé," Eve observed as the young woman took a small compact out of her purse, opened it, and blotted her nose with the sponge.

"Well, it isn't actually official," she replied, reaching back into the purse and taking out a tube of lipstick.

Eve waited.

"His divorce isn't exactly finalized." She opened the tube and slid it across her lips. They were stained a dark red.

Eve was fascinated. She hadn't watched a woman put on makeup since she was a girl watching her younger sister. Unlike

Eve, who had never used any products on her face, Dorisanne loved wearing makeup.

"He's still married then?" she asked, watching as Megan blotted her lips with a tissue.

The young woman stopped what she was doing. There was a long sigh from her. "Officially, he is still married, but that marriage has been dead a long time."

Eve turned to Daniel, who gave a slight shrug.

"How old are you, Megan?" Eve asked.

"Twenty-three," came the reply.

"And how old is Chaz?"

"Forty-eight or forty-nine," she answered.

"Actually, Mr. Cheston is fifty-three," Daniel interjected, watching her in the rearview mirror.

Eve looked at Megan to catch her reaction, but she didn't seem to care about her mistake.

"What's a Hollywood director doing in New Mexico anyway?" she asked.

Daniel answered, "Haven't you heard that we're the new favorite movie location? All the young actors are buying up land around St. John's and Tesuque. Everybody here thinks they can be a star. Shoot, I was even going to see if I could stand in for Denzel Washington when he was here making that movie last summer."

Evangeline laughed.

"Why you laughing? Don't you think I look like Denzel?"

"Daniel, I told you, I'm a nun. We don't have movie night at the monastery. I don't know what Denzel Washington looks like anymore."

He sat up, facing straight ahead, giving Evangeline a good view of his profile. "Looks just like this." He held his head high, pointed at his chin, and grinned.

Evangeline rolled her eyes and shook her head.

"He was here because he's supposed to be finishing up some details for a feature they're planning to film over in Madrid," Megan piped up.

"And exactly how long has he been missing?" Eve wanted to know.

"Six and a half days," Megan replied.

"Where was he before he came to Madrid?" Eve had turned and was looking over her shoulder at the passenger in the backseat.

"He was at the Betty Ford Center."

Eve eyed Daniel.

"Chaz sometimes has problems with a few substances."

Eve nodded. "Could he be having one of those problems again?"

"No, he was clean this time for sure."

Daniel glanced over at Eve and lifted his eyebrows.

"So when did you get involved in this?" she asked the driver.

"The Captain called me a couple of days ago to see if there had been any news at the station."

"Like whether or not anybody else was looking for him too?"

"That and to check out a few things." He glanced once more in the rearview mirror at Megan, and Eve understood that he had been asked to do some research on the young starlet.

"Anybody remember seeing him around Madrid lately?"

Megan seemed to be studying Evangeline. "You know, you sound just like your dad," she noted. "He asked all these questions too."

Eve turned back around in her seat and gazed out the windshield.

"She's right, you know," Daniel added. "He's always thought you had good instincts, thought you should have given law enforcement a chance." Daniel turned on his signal, taking the ramp off the interstate to St. Francis Street.

"He said you had a good nose for crime," Megan noted. "He said when you were little, you were always asking him about his cases, wanting to know how murders happened, who the suspects were. He thought you would be a police officer."

Evangeline looked first at Daniel and then back at Megan. It was unnerving hearing first a family friend and then a stranger tell her something that had been said about her that she didn't know. In all her years growing up under the thumb of Captain Jack Divine, he had never told her what he had apparently told his partner and a virtual stranger.

"Of course, he's happy you became a nun," Megan said.

Eve made no reply. She was clearly uncomfortable talking about her vocation choices with these two. Besides, she knew that wasn't completely true. The Captain had not argued with his daughter when she made her announcement to join the order, but he obviously was not happy about it.

They stopped at the traffic light and could see the hospital just ahead.

"What are all those news vans and police cars doing at St. Vincent's?" Eve asked.

Daniel made the turn and started into the hospital parking lot.

"Oh, dear God! Stop the car! It's them!" came the cry from the backseat.

Daniel hit the brakes.

"It's who?" Eve yelled, bracing herself against the dashboard.

Once the car came to a complete stop, Daniel and Eve both turned to the passenger in the back.

"Victoria and Charles Jr.," she replied.

The two in the front waited. These were not names they knew.

"His family," she added. "Chaz's wife and son."

And they turned back to look ahead at the woman and young man being escorted into the hospital through the emergency-room doors.

SIX

"You get hold of Dorisanne?" Daniel had gotten a cup of coffee from the refreshment cart that was pushed against the wall in the surgical waiting area. He had taken Megan back to her hotel and then joined Eve in the waiting room. She was out of her habit and dressed in jeans, a long-sleeved T-shirt, and a leather jacket, although she did still keep a rosary in her front pocket that she fidgets with.

She nodded.

"Is she coming home?" he asked, taking a seat beside Eve.

She shook her head, recalling the conversation she had with her younger sister. "She said she just got a new job at the Rio, doesn't have any time off yet."

Daniel didn't respond. Dorisanne hadn't been back to New Mexico since her mother's funeral. She had stayed in Madrid for almost a year, serving as the primary caregiver while Eve was in Pecos and Jackson worked on the force. It hadn't been an easy time for anyone.

"She still dancing?" he asked, knowing the young woman's dream.

Eve shook her head. "Cocktail waitress," she answered. "Apparently, there's some marriage trouble." She paused, thinking about Dorisanne's husband, Robbie, and the stories she had heard of gambling debts and an unsavory group of friends.

"Jackson tried to warn her," Daniel commented. His jaw tightened.

Eve turned to the man and made no response. They both knew how that conversation went. Captain Jack and his youngest daughter hadn't spoken to each other in years.

"She says it's my time to take care of a parent," she said. "Claims I'm the only one he'll listen to anyway."

Daniel smiled. "Well, you do seem to get more out of him than your sister ever did." He leaned in to her. "You up for the task?"

"Taking care of the Captain?" She shook her head. "That's not a task, that's a calling." She glanced around the waiting room. Family members and friends of surgical patients filled the seats. How many of them were not just hoping for good news but were also making plans for the changes about to take place in their lives?

She studied the faces of the people her age and wondered if any of them were in shock about a parent's need for surgery, if they felt the way she did when she got the news that the Captain was losing his leg. She wondered if they were facing the same struggle of how to provide care for an aging parent.

She decided to change the subject. "How did Megan take the news?"

Eve had heard that the missing director was found dead, and she was curious about the young starlet's state of mind. It had been confirmed that Charles Cheston's body was found earlier in the day up around Cerrillos, near the old mines. His family was already in town, having filed their own missing person's report. They were downstairs viewing the body, confirming the identity of the victim. Somehow the news had been leaked, and every media outlet from across the state had taken up residence in the hospital parking lot.

"She wanted to see him," Daniel replied. "I asked if she could get in, but several of the officers said that only immediate family was being allowed into the area. I think she tried earlier."

"My guess is that the wife wouldn't be all that hospitable to her husband's mistress."

"From what the officers assigned to the family say, that's an understatement for sure."

Eve nodded.

A volunteer came into the waiting room, called out a name, and Eve and Daniel watched as four or five people got up from their seats and followed her.

"Was it foul play?" Eve asked.

Daniel shrugged. "Found at the bottom of a ravine, no signs of struggle, no gunshot wounds, no stabbing. Hard to say. But his car wasn't there, and he certainly wasn't dressed to be out on any hike."

"You think he was dumped?"

"I'd need more information, but I'd say it's likely that's the case."

"Is she a suspect?" Eve asked, referring to Megan.

Daniel understood the reference. "Aren't all mistresses suspects?"

Eve thought about growing up in the home of a police officer, how she loved to hear the reports of homicides and stories of crime. Her mother and sister hated it when the Captain would start to talk about the events of his day, the details of a local murder, but Eve had always enjoyed hearing the inside information.

"Eight out of ten times, the victim knows the perp," he used to say. "Be more worried about the folks you have a relationship with than you are about strangers." And Eve used to wonder if that bit of advice included parents as well.

"What else do you know about the guy? Who did he hang out with?"

He shook his head. "I don't know."

She nodded, looking up at the clock to check the time. She had been waiting for over four hours.

"You talk to your boss?" Daniel asked.

"I called the vice superior after I talked to Dorisanne. I can take as long as I need," she said, then paused. "You know, maybe it'll actually be good for me to get away for a little while." She slid her hands down the front of her legs and stretched them out. She felt so much more comfortable dressed in her old clothes.

Daniel studied her and was about to ask another question when the volunteer walked back into the waiting room. They both turned to hear the name.

"Divine," the older woman wearing a bright pink lab coat called out.

"It's *Diveen*," Eve answered sharply. She stood, blew out a breath, and made the sign of the cross in repentance, immediately regretting the tone of her voice.

SEVEN

————— ✤✤✤ —————

"You look like death warmed over," the voice bellowed. Evangeline was quickly roused from her sleep. "Why aren't you wearing your nun's gown? And how's the dog?"

She shook her head and rubbed her eyes. The clock was mounted on the wall above a whiteboard that listed the names of a nurse and tech and a goal for the day: "no pain and begin physical therapy." It was six o'clock, but Evangeline couldn't tell whether it was morning or night. She glanced over at the patient.

She answered when she finally felt clear. "Trooper is at Daniel's. And it's called a habit, and I'm not wearing it because I'm not on duty right now, and I look like this because I've been sleeping in a chair while you're in a comfortable bed."

"What makes you think this bed is comfortable?" Jackson asked, trying to shift his weight and grimacing with the movement. "And I thought nuns were always on duty."

She watched him, choosing not to respond to the comment about her clothes and her vocation. "You okay?" she asked.

"Do I look okay?" He tried pushing himself up in the bed.

Evangeline got up and moved over to the Captain. "Here, there's a button for that." She reached for the side railing and pressed a small image of a bed with arrows facing up. The top of the bed began to rise.

"Not too much, not too much!" he shouted.

Evangeline released the button and sighed. "Better?"

He nodded.

"What day is this?" he asked.

Evangeline went over to the window, opened the blinds, and could see the sun rising in the east. *Morning*, she thought. "It's the third day," she answered.

"The third day after the surgery or the third day being in the hospital?"

She turned to him. "Aren't they the same?"

"No," he griped. "If you count the day of surgery and it's been three days since that day, then it's the fourth day of being in the hospital. If you aren't counting the surgery day as a hospital day, which if I recall the operation was in the afternoon, then it's just the third day of being in the hospital, two days after the surgery."

There was a pause.

Evangeline stood at the window a bit longer and then returned to her seat and sat down. "It's Wednesday," she said. "The surgery was Monday afternoon." She hesitated briefly. "That makes this two days after the surgery, almost three full days in the hospital. You were in the intensive care unit until Tuesday night because you wouldn't wake up and were moved to this floor when you did. This is the third day I've been here. The nurses let me take a shower yesterday, and I've eaten three daily specials in the cafeteria. I slept in the surgical waiting room Monday night and the intensive care unit waiting room most of Tuesday night. There are recliners in the intensive care unit waiting area but not in the surgical one. I had a pillow and a thin blanket that a Navajo woman brought me late on the first night but wanted it back yesterday. I stayed in the waiting rooms and moved in here when you were transferred." She closed her eyes and shook her head, mad at herself for being so easily provoked. She took a breath to start again.

"It's three days in the hospital, two days since your surgery."

Jackson Divine stared at his daughter. He waited. "That's all I wanted to know."

She didn't respond.

"Why are you being so snippy? I thought that was why you wanted to be a nun, to quit being so snippy."

"I'm not being snippy," she replied. "I'm just answering your question. And I didn't become a nun to quit being snippy."

"Why don't you go back to Pecos?" he asked. "The surgery's over. I don't need you here all the time."

"Well, thanks for the gratitude," she said.

"You know what I mean," he said, trying to make amends. "I'm fine. I'll call you when I get discharged. You can come to the house and help me get settled."

Evangeline studied the man. She knew this was only the beginning of an inevitable and interminable battle she was destined to have with the Captain. In the three days she had been with him, she had not told him about the leave of absence she'd been given by the monastery. She had not told him about the long conversation she'd had with the nurses and doctors at the hospital. She had not explained that she was there for more than just the hospital stay. They had not discussed the fact that she was going to be his primary caregiver for the next two months. It wasn't yet time.

"You've missed quite a lot of action while you've been dosed up on the morphine."

He waited.

"I met Megan Flint," she said.

He seemed surprised at the mention of the young woman's name but didn't say a word.

"She came with Daniel to Pecos."

He made no response.

"And they found her boyfriend."

He seemed to perk up at that announcement.

"He's dead," she added.

The Captain's head jerked up, and he opened his mouth as if to make a remark, but before either of them could speak, the door swung open and a young nurse walked in.

EIGHT

——— ❦ ———

"Good morning, Mr. Divine, and you are up early today," the nurse called out cheerfully. Her singsong voice reminded Eve of a kindergarten teacher.

"*Diveen*," both Jackson and Evangeline blurted out, correcting her.

"Right, I'm sorry." She cleared her throat. "Mr. Divine, it's good to see you this morning, and I'm glad you still have family here with you," she announced.

Evangeline smiled but didn't say anything.

Jackson rolled his eyes. He was not happy for the intrusion. His mood shifted. He made a kind of growl.

"So, did we sleep okay?" the nurse asked.

Evangeline braced for the reply. She knew how the Captain hated being spoken to like a child.

"I slept like a man who just had his leg cut off and is confined to a bed that's wrapped in plastic. I can't attest for the one down there trying to stretch out in a hardback chair after a couple of nights sleeping in a waiting room or for you." He looked up at his attendant. "I can only speak for myself in reply to your question that apparently was addressed to all of us gathered in this room. I don't know how *we* slept, only how *I* slept. And that was not all that fabulous."

The nurse appeared stunned by her patient's comment and turned to Evangeline.

She just shook her head. "He's not a morning person," she explained, settling back in her chair. "And to answer your question, he slept on and off through the night."

The young woman tried to smile. "Well, okay," she said, her voice a bit softer. "My name is Tina and I'll be your nurse today," she continued as she pulled on a pair of latex gloves. "Raymond is your nurse tech, and he'll be in shortly to help you with your morning meds and a bath, maybe a shave, if you'd like."

She squeezed the bottoms of the bags of fluid hanging on the IV pole beside the bed, punched a few numbers into the machine keypad, attended to the IV site on the patient's left arm, and then walked down to the end of the bed. She pulled back the sheet and checked the bandage around where Mr. Divine's leg had been amputated. She poked and prodded a bit.

Evangeline noticed how her father turned away when she did.

"Well, there's no drainage from your site," the nurse explained. She felt for a pulse in the top of his thigh. "That's a good thing," she noted. "That means the wound is healing like we want." She felt for a pulse in his other leg, down near the ankle. "We have physical therapy coming in this afternoon," she said, pulling the sheet over his leg. "They're going to try and help you get some strength back in your upper body, have you do some exercises while you're in the bed. And we're going to start working on getting you ready for a prosthetic." She smiled. "The wound is healing nicely. The swelling in your residual limb is decreasing. Your vitals are good and your blood sugar has been only slightly higher for the last twenty-four hours. So you are well on your way," she added.

She looked down at her patient. "Is there anything you need this morning? How's the pain? Do you need more morphine?"

"No," he answered. "The pain is manageable. I'd just like some coffee," he said. "And the morning paper."

Tina was still smiling. She moved over to the whiteboard and erased the name Phyllis before writing in her own. She seemed to be studying the day's goal, trying to decide whether or not to change it, and then put down the marker.

"Dietary will be delivering the breakfast trays shortly," she responded. "They usually come around seven o'clock on this floor. Hopefully you asked for coffee when you filled out your menu request yesterday." She smoothed down the front of her uniform.

"And as for the news," she said, turning to face her patient, "I can go ahead and tell you this morning's headlines." She raised her eyebrows as if she were delivering a great announcement. "It turns out that the Hollywood director was murdered," she said, recapping the report that had been blaring across television screens all morning. "The one who received an Academy Award and was cheating on his wife."

She walked over to the trash can by the sink. "Everybody thinks it was Megan Flint who killed him."

Both Captain Divine and Evangeline snapped to full attention.

The nurse yanked off her gloves, dropped them in the trash, and started to head out the door. Just before leaving, she turned back, apparently enjoying her position as the center of his attention. "She's here in Santa Fe too."

There was a nod, accenting her announcement like an exclamation point, and before Captain Divine or his daughter could utter a reply or ask a question, Nurse Tina was gone.

NINE

The Captain had made the therapist stay an extra hour, asking for more exercises, pushing himself as hard as he could until he had finally driven himself to exhaustion. When the therapist left, appearing almost as tired as her patient, he dropped off to sleep. Evangeline quietly slipped from the room and took a much-needed ride on her Harley. After her breather from the hospital, she decided she would go down to the chapel and say her morning prayers.

Glancing at her watch as she got off the bike after her return, though, she realized it was well past noon. Perhaps she should say Sext or None instead. She pushed down the bike stand and kicked the dirt from her boots. She smoothed down her shirt and stuck her hands in the pockets of her jeans, glad to be out of the long dress she had become accustomed to wearing. She was grateful that Daniel had taken her back to Pecos, giving her the opportunity to retrieve the Harley. She knew the bike was the only thing that would keep her sane with her new duty as caregiver. She could pray and read sacred texts and chant like the monks, but riding the Harley remained her favorite religious experience.

Evangeline felt better as she walked back into the hospital. Sliding her fingers through her mussed hair, she hoped Daniel wasn't around to question her about the helmet. She reached for her rosary in the front pocket of her jacket and held it in her hand. She was thinking about the Captain and the talk she wouldn't be able to postpone much longer.

She was rehearsing it in her mind—how she'd tell him that she was going home with him. He would claim he didn't need help, but after talking to the doctor and being with her dad since the operation, she knew differently. Just like Dorisanne had told her on the phone, it was her turn to take care of their parent. She had not been there for her mother; she was going to have to make up for that by being there for him. Besides, the arrangements had already been made. The day after the surgery she had gone back to Pecos, gotten her things, and moved back into her childhood home in Madrid. The Captain was just going to have to deal with the situation.

She was almost at the chapel when she noticed a group of people gathered near a side entrance, four or five adults huddled close together, with a security guard and a couple of other hospital employees standing nearby. A police officer was positioned in front of the group of people who were not wearing uniforms.

Evangeline stopped. The voices were so loud she couldn't help but overhear the conversation.

"We do not have all the answers at this time." Apparently the police officer had just arrived at the scene and was only beginning to try to explain the situation. "You're going to have to wait until there is a final report from the autopsy. All we know is that it is now officially being investigated as a homicide."

"Now a homicide?" a woman shouted. "We knew when they found his body it was a homicide. Why did it take you so long to figure that out?" She was middle-aged, late forties maybe, auburn hair twisted into a tight knot, petite. Even watching from a distance, it was clear to Evangeline that this was a woman used to having her way.

The officer sighed. "I'm just trying to give you the facts as we know them. When we brought the body here three days ago, we weren't even sure of an exact time of death, much less the cause."

"I don't need an exact time of death, and I don't need to know details of what killed him. I just need to know when we can probate the will and move forward with this . . ." She paused. "This mess." She was wearing sunglasses, a white fur coat, white leggings, and brown boots. A gold purse dangled from her arm.

"Well, I don't have an answer to that. Again, all I can give you is the fact that it is now officially a murder investigation," he explained.

It was easy for Evangeline to see that the police officer was frustrated. He was young, probably a rookie, she thought, sent by his more experienced partner to deal with the dead man's family. She glanced out the large plate-glass windows and door that opened into a side parking lot and noticed two black-and-white city-police vehicles as well as a few television news vans. It appeared that most of the media had lost interest and gone back to their stations.

"We have not stayed around this cowboy town for three days

just to hear something we already knew." The dark-haired young man who was speaking stepped closer to the officer. "We expect you to have more answers for us about my father. Where's your supervisor?" He was small, maybe mid-twenties, and dressed in jeans and a leather jacket.

Evangeline moved closer and leaned in. She wanted to hear the officer's response so that she could report the conversation accurately. She knew the Captain would love hearing about this hospital-lobby event.

The officer placed his hands on the items bulging from his belt, a holster and a radio clip. "He's back at the station." He raised his chin but kept his emotions under control. "Did you get the autopsy report?" he asked.

"Of course we got the autopsy report," the young man answered. He stepped back and reached over to take the hand of the petite woman standing at his side. He took a breath and the woman dropped his hand.

"How soon will his body be released?" This came from an older man standing on the other side of the woman. He also stepped forward, and Evangeline could see that he was wearing a black suit, a black overcoat, and a striped tie. He was tall and was holding a briefcase in one hand. He looked like a lawyer.

"I don't know. I haven't been informed of when that will happen," he said. The police officer glanced over in Evangeline's direction. Realizing she had been caught eavesdropping, she didn't move.

The police officer stared for a second, and Evangeline quickly looked away. She felt her face redden and knew she had been listening to the private conversation too long. She figured she should leave the area and go into the chapel to pray, but the truth was she was too enthralled at what was being said. It was clear that this was the family of the dead man—the wife and son Megan had seen when they first got to the hospital. Now Eve was getting the chance to see them up close.

"And are we free to go home?" the woman wanted to know.

The officer didn't respond.

Evangeline stayed where she was, pretending to read the sign posted by the chapel door. She looked down at her clothes, thinking that it might have been better if she were still in her habit. Perhaps, dressed as a nun, she would not be as noticeable standing where she was. She began to question her decision to leave her habit at the monastery.

"Look, all of us have been questioned, me, our son, his producer, our friends . . ." The woman hesitated and Evangeline peeked around, trying to get a better look at who was speaking.

"It's humiliating," she continued. "None of us had anything to do with any homicide. Maybe you should talk to the people in that godforsaken, hippie town where he was staying. Or to one of the young girls he keeps finding at rehab or in a bar and always puts in his films. Did you talk to that trashy blonde he's been with?"

Someone tried to hush the woman. Their voices seemed to lower. Evangeline could no longer make out what they were saying and knew that if she wanted to be able to hear more, she would have to move closer to the gathering. She started to head in their direction and stopped. *What am I doing?* she asked herself. She needed to pray. She reached for her rosary.

She was moving back toward the chapel and away from the

conversation that had captured her attention when she spotted a door opening beside her. With a quick step to the right, she moved aside to keep it from slamming into her.

Without a word of greeting or apology, a security guard hurried through, the door closing slowly. She was about to say something to the man about how he should watch where he was going, but then she saw another security guard and a young woman walking behind him. She could see into the corridor as the door was closing that the woman was petite, had long, blond hair falling below a large black hat, and was wearing a full-length red coat, black boots, and sunglasses. It was Megan.

The first guard hurriedly walked past the nun and over to where the dead man's family was gathered with the police officer. He disappeared from Evangeline's line of sight, but before she knew it, he was heading back in her direction. He opened the door beside her and once again headed down the corridor.

Evangeline hesitated only a second. She had to find out what Megan was doing. She pocketed her rosary and opened the door to the hallway that the guard had just reentered. Quietly, she slipped into the passageway after him.

TEN

Eve followed as Megan Flint and the security guards made their way down the stairs and along several corridors. She wanted to call out to Megan, let her know that she was there, but they were walking too fast. Raising her voice might cause a scene. Eve caught up with them just as they moved through two swinging doors, which had windows that allowed her to see Megan Flint and the men move toward a table in the center of the room covered in a white sheet. Eve stopped short. She didn't want to intrude on a private moment, and she wasn't all that thrilled about going into that part of the hospital.

One of the guards pulled down the sheet, exposing a head and torso. Megan draped herself over the body, placing her face next to the dead man's. The guard looked away awkwardly while the woman wept and appeared to be speaking softly to the dead man. Evangeline felt in her pocket for the rosary and was about to say prayers on the man's behalf. She bowed her head.

"Hey you!"

Eve was so startled she fell forward and bumped her head on the swinging doors. One of the two guards hurried over and pulled the doors open. Eve strained to keep from falling forward and watched as the rosary dropped from her hands.

"What are you doing down here?"

Eve was unsteady; she reached up to rub her head and took a step inside the room.

"I . . . I . . ." She was having some difficulty putting together a sentence. She reached down and picked up her rosary. When she stood up, the man was standing right beside her, leaning over her. She balled up a fist and was ready to take a swing. The Captain had taught her basic self-defense moves when she was a teenager. Not since she was sixteen and punched a boy for taunting Dorisanne had she actually gotten in a fight, but her instincts were still intact. A voice called out from inside the room: "Eve?" It was Megan.

Eve didn't respond. The security guards, both the one standing near the body and the one standing over her, waited. The one standing over her wore a hospital uniform. His nameplate read Stanley and Eve had to smile. Even though he had seemed threatening at first, she had never met a Stanley she couldn't take down.

"Sister Eve, what are you doing down here?" Megan asked, walking over to where Eve stood.

"I saw you upstairs and followed you down here," she replied, smiling at Stanley and relaxing her hands. "Are you okay?" Eve asked.

The young woman nodded. "I just wanted to see him," she replied, looking back at the body. "They wouldn't let me see him before now."

Eve nodded.

"This your sister?" Stanley asked.

Both women shook their heads.

"She's a nun; she's that kind of sister," Megan explained.

Stanley and the other security guard seemed skeptical, and once again Eve questioned her decision not to wear her habit.

"Her father is a patient upstairs." Megan turned to Eve. "How is Captain Divine doing?" she asked.

Eve smiled. "Better," she answered. "He's out of intensive care now, and he's back to his grouchy self."

The security guard closest to the table cleared his throat, and Megan turned her attention back to the dead man, nodding. "I know, I know," she said. She wiped her eyes and nose, glancing over to Eve. "We can't stay long." She reached under the white sheet and took the dead man's hand. She started to cry again, and the others in the room looked away.

Eve reached into her pocket for her rosary but couldn't find it. She looked around on the floor and then remembered she had placed it in her other pocket. She took it out, closed her eyes, fingered the beads, and then looked up, getting a clear view of the dead man. Megan had pulled out his hand and seemed to be trying to feel for something on his wrist. Eve then closed her eyes to pray.

"Are you saying a prayer?" Megan asked.

Eve opened her eyes. "The rosary," she answered. "I'm saying the rosary."

Megan nodded. "That's nice," she said, and then paused a second. "Can you say it out loud?"

Eve looked at the two guards. The one standing near them

made the sign of the cross and dropped his eyes while Stanley blew out a long breath.

She moved closer to the young woman. "I believe in God, the Father Almighty—" She began reciting the Apostles' Creed but was interrupted.

"Look, we can't stay for all that. We have to go," Stanley announced. "We can't be here any longer. If they find out we let you down here, we could lose our jobs." He glared at the other guard.

Eve looked over at Megan, who was nodding, the tears flowing down her cheeks. She took her by the hand.

"I'll need to take you out the back door," the one standing near them said. "It's not that far and I'll call ahead and make sure your driver is nearby. That way we can get you out of here before anybody in the family or any of those reporters spot you."

Megan wiped her eyes and pushed her hair behind her ears. "There are reporters here?" she asked, suddenly sounding interested.

Stanley nodded. "Most left, but there are a couple here since the latest news came out," he replied. "Somebody leaked the information that your boyfriend was murdered. They circled their wagons hours ago."

Megan seemed to be considering the situation. The security guard near her took her by the elbow, but she yanked it away.

"I've changed my mind," she said. "I'd like to visit Mr. Divine before I go," she added, surprising Evangeline as much as the guards.

ELEVEN

—— ✦ ——

"Bad idea, lady," Stanley responded, standing his ground and shaking his shaved head from side to side.

He was short, fit, and square, with the appearance of a young soldier. He stood upright, lifting his chin, dropping his arms to his sides, readying himself for a fight. He was dressed all in black—a dark, long-sleeved T-shirt, the hospital logo embroidered on the small pocket under the nameplate, and black cargo pants. "The family is right upstairs in the lobby," he said. "The reporters are just outside the front doors. I've got an officer watching Mrs. Cheston and her son, and he'll let us know if they leave the premises. But right now, I'm pretty sure they'd see you if you walked up or took an elevator to the lobby. And if they see you again, I'm also pretty sure that the wife will have another fit."

Evangeline recalled Daniel mentioning the attempt to get Megan in when the body was first brought to the hospital. She hadn't heard but now assumed that there had been a confrontation between Megan and the dead man's wife.

"Thomas," Megan said, speaking to the guard standing beside her, "they may have the right to try and keep me from being with Chaz in the emergency department or here in the morgue, but they cannot stop me from visiting a friend who happens to be a patient in this hospital."

She pulled her sunglasses from the large purse sitting by her feet. "They don't have control over the entire facility, do they?" She looked at Stanley.

Evangeline wanted to get out of the morgue and back to the Captain. Alone. She wished she had never eavesdropped on a conversation she had no business listening to and then followed Megan down to the morgue.

"They don't, do they, Tommy?" Megan asked again.

He looked up at his colleague for assistance, but the other guy just shook his head. It was clearly not his idea to be down here in the first place.

"They can't keep me from visiting someone else in this hospital, can they?"

Tommy softened and Stanley pushed open the doors and walked out. He was having no part of this.

"No," Tommy answered. "They can't stop you from being in the hospital, only from seeing their family member. But I still don't think—"

"Fine," she interrupted him. "I would like to visit Captain Divine." She turned to Evangeline, who was trying not to meet her eyes. "I'd like to say hello to your father, Sister Eve. Would that be all right?"

Evangeline didn't know how to answer. She looked at

Thomas, the security guard, who seemed to be trying to direct her to say no.

"I won't stay long," Megan pleaded. "I like your dad. I think it would be nice just to pop in and say hello."

Evangeline glanced away from the man and turned to Megan. "He's sleeping," she said.

"Oh," the young woman responded, her voice suddenly small and childlike. "I understand," she added.

"Okay, then." The security guard took over. "To get you out of here, we'll go out these doors and around to the back of the kitchen. I'll walk you through there and out the rear entrance. I'm pretty sure if we hurry, nobody will see us."

Megan dropped her head. Even wearing the sunglasses, it was easy to see she was crying again.

Evangeline thought about the guard's instructions. After finally being allowed a few minutes to see the man she loved, Megan was being pushed to go through the kitchen and out the rear door, like a servant or trash or . . . "I believe in God . . ." She began the prayer again, and then she stopped. She couldn't stand for a person to be treated like that.

"We can wake him up," she said, dropping the rosary into her pocket, abandoning the prayer and surprising the guard and the young woman and especially herself.

The two were just starting to head past her. Thomas was getting ready to push open the door.

They paused as Eve said, "I'm sure he'd like to see you. A visit would brighten his spirits."

The young woman lifted her chin and raised her shoulders.

Evangeline forced a smile.

Thomas shook his head before he moved away from them through the exit and reached for his radio to make a call.

Megan grabbed Evangeline by the arm, waiting for the guard to give his permission and to escort the two women. "We can wake him up," she repeated with a smile, pleased that she would be walking through the hospital, through the main doors, through the occupied corridors, and not out of it through the rear entrance.

After making his call, Thomas walked back into the room where the two women were waiting and opened the door. It was easy to see that he was not happy at all.

TWELVE

Evangeline could hear him barking orders to someone before they were even out of the elevator and onto the floor. Clearly, the Captain was no longer asleep. She was about to apologize to the young woman for his behavior but then changed her mind. If Megan Flint really wanted to see the private detective she'd employed while he was in the hospital, then she would see the man in all his fullness, she decided.

"How did you come to hire the Captain?" Evangeline asked as they rounded the nurses' station.

It was just the two of them walking together since the security guard did not escort them beyond the bank of elevators on the bottom floor. He asked Evangeline for her father's room number and then simply reached in, pressed the button to the floor where Captain Divine was a patient, stepped out, and nodded his good-bye. Just like that, the door closed and the two women were alone in the elevator. Evangeline wasn't sure about Megan, but she was very relieved when it sailed right past the lobby and straight up to the floor.

"It's funny that you call him 'the Captain,'" Megan noted. "When did that start?"

Eve shrugged. "My sister and I started calling him that when we were really young. He was quite the authoritarian in our home. Our mother tried to make us stop, but it just sort of stuck."

The door opened and the two stepped out.

"I didn't really have a father, so I don't know what I'd call one," she said. "I call my mother by her first name, Lou Anne," she added softly. "I take care of Lou Anne. She's in a facility in California. She's . . ." Megan hesitated. "She's not well."

Eve just nodded. She wasn't sure why Megan was telling her this, but hearing about the absent father and the plight of the young woman's mother softened her view of the movie star.

"Anyway"—Megan cleared her throat—"to answer your question, I came to Santa Fe the day Chaz was supposed to be back in L.A. I was waiting for him at the airport to give him a change of clothes for his meetings." She had stuck her arm through Evangeline's and was walking beside her as if they were old friends.

"The pilot who was supposed to pick up Chaz said he waited two hours and then finally went ahead and made the flight without him. I knew something was wrong immediately and had him turn around and fly me here."

They stopped as they turned down the hall that led to the Captain's room.

"And he did?" Evangeline asked, facing Megan. The ease with which this young woman could apparently get what she wanted surprised her.

"Well, he called Mr. Polland first. He's Chaz's producer," she explained. "When he found out that Chaz had not arrived in California, he was all too glad to have the pilot bring me back here." She leaned in to Evangeline, speaking in a whisper. "The studio has a lot of money invested in Chaz's next picture. He wanted him found almost as much as I did."

"So, you came to Santa Fe, and . . . ?" Evangeline was curious.

"And I got a driver and went to Madrid and out to the house he was renting." She paused. "Isn't it funny that you pronounce *Madrid* that way instead of Madrid, like the town in Spain?" She waved away the stray thought. "Anyway, I had come here with him a couple of times last fall, so I knew my way around," she added with a sigh.

They continued walking down the hall, nearing the room.

"And I waited there for a day and decided something must have happened to Chaz. He just wouldn't disappear like that, not without calling me." She removed her arm from Evangeline's and took off her sunglasses, then reached into her purse for a tube of lipstick and a mirrored compact. She studied her reflection, dabbed under her eyes, painted on the dark red balm, smacked her lips together, and returned the items to her purse. She smiled at Evangeline, who was watching, and went on. "The last time I was here, I met your dad at that local bar where everybody hangs out." She stopped briefly. "The Mine Tunnel?" she asked.

"Shaft," Evangeline answered, knowing the place quite well. "The Mineshaft."

"Right. I just love that little place," she said, grinning. "It's so quaint."

Evangeline nodded. She thought about explaining that Marcie

Lunez, the owner, was an old and dear friend of the family, but before she could do so, Megan continued.

"After Chaz didn't show up and the police were no help at all, I located Captain Divine's office near the fire station and asked for his help."

Evangeline glanced at the door to his room.

"I guess he started the ball rolling for the search by filing a missing person's report with the police. He has a lot of friends there," she noted, as if Evangeline hadn't heard. "And then Chaz's wife, Victoria, called them. Mr. Polland called. After a few days, everybody in Hollywood was dialing up the Santa Fe police, supposedly looking for him. But your dad and I were searching the entire state long before anybody else bothered to show up."

"So, you were here in New Mexico all last week?" Evangeline asked, calculating how much time the Captain had spent with his most recent client.

"Yes, I guess so. I was with your father late last week and over the weekend. Then I came back on Monday, and that's when we went to the clinic and then here."

Evangeline nodded. They were just outside the door when all of a sudden the nursing assistant came running out. She was startled to see the two women, immediately recognized Evangeline as the daughter of the patient, and was about to complain about her father, when she took a closer look at Megan.

"Oh, my!" she said and fell back into the room.

THIRTEEN

"You're . . ." The nursing assistant was at a loss for words. "You're . . . you're that movie star?" She had regained her balance and was standing before them. The door to the room had pushed her forward. Her eyes were wide with excitement. "I love your work!"

Megan smiled and held out her hand. "I'm Megan Flint," she introduced herself. Her tone was humble, her kindness genuine.

"I know!" the hospital employee exclaimed. "I loved you in *Too Far Away*!" Her face reddened. She reached out and took the young woman's extended hand.

"That was a very special movie for me too," Megan replied. "Thank you so much."

"I can't believe you're here!" She yanked Megan into a big hug.

"Oh, well, thank you." Megan tried to pull away, startled by the overwhelming affection.

As Evangeline watched the encounter, it all began to make sense: the hat and sunglasses, the way Megan could so easily get what she wanted from hospital security guards, the stares from the women at the nurses' station as they passed. Megan Flint wasn't just a beautiful woman. She wasn't just a client and the girlfriend of a Hollywood director. She was a celebrity.

Eve had forgotten about that role in society. In her years at the convent, she had become unfamiliar with how people longed for fame, longed to be in the limelight, longed to be close to those who were famous. She watched Megan and realized that kind of pressure must be somewhat intense, maybe even unwelcome.

"What are you doing here?" the nursing assistant asked. "You aren't sick, are you? Oh, please tell me you aren't sick!"

Megan shook her head and held her hand to her chest. "Oh, no," she answered, drawing out the word *no*.

"Well, that's a relief," the woman responded.

An angry voice bellowed from behind them, "Do you mind?"

"You're not related to him, are you?" She pointed behind her and rolled her eyes. "Because if you are, then you have my sympathies." She seemed to realize once again that Evangeline was standing right there.

"Oh, I'm sorry, Ms. Divine." She was clearly embarrassed.

Evangeline took in a breath, calming herself. "It's *Diveen*," she explained.

"Right, I'm sorry."

Evangeline nodded and the three women stood together awkwardly at the door.

"Oh, goodness, what am I thinking? Can I have your autograph, Miss Flint?" the nursing assistant asked. She patted her pockets, searching for a piece of paper, and then held open the chart she was holding and a pen.

Evangeline could see that the young movie star was being asked to sign her autograph in her father's medical chart, on a progress note, to be exact. She was about to point out the inappropriateness of such a request when the Captain yelled once more for the chit-chat in the hall to be done elsewhere.

Megan quickly signed her name and handed over the pen to her fan. "Thank you for all the good work you do here at the hospital," she said, her voice thick and sugary.

"Oh, it's a pleasure," the nursing assistant responded.

The Captain yelled again and she closed the chart.

"Well, I mean, most of the time," she said, whispering. "I guess I need to go." She backed away from the door and the two women. "It's so nice to meet you," she added.

"Can't you please take it somewhere else?" The patient's voice was loud enough for others in the hall to hear.

Everyone standing around in the corridor and at the nurses' station at the other end stopped and stared in the direction of the three women.

"I better go," the nursing assistant whispered. "Thank you so much. Thank you."

"You're welcome," Megan said, touching the woman on the arm.

"Well," Evangeline noted as the hospital employee quickly hurried away, "we're in luck! I'd say he's awake."

And the two of them headed into the room.

FOURTEEN

"I told you that I don't drink decaf!" the man growled as the door opened.

"Well, maybe decaf's not such a bad idea," Evangeline responded as she entered with Megan, closing the door behind them. She moved over to his bedside.

"I thought you were that ridiculous excuse for a nurse."

"Do you think you might tone it down just a bit?"

"That girl tried to give me the wrong medication!" he yelled. "She could have killed me!"

Evangeline rolled her eyes. "You don't have to scream. And she's not the nurse, she's the nursing assistant."

He placed his arm across his forehead and closed his eyes. "Well, that explains why she doesn't know what she's doing. Why do the nurses need assistants? Can't they do their own jobs? Who was doing all the talking? I'm trying to take a nap."

"I think you know Miss Flint," Evangeline said, motioning their guest forward.

"Oh, Jackson," the young woman said, moving over to the bed and taking him by the hand. "I'm so sorry you've been hospitalized."

Evangeline was surprised by the transformation. She had never seen her father so affected by a woman. The reaction was not at all what she expected. He smiled at the visitor, turned quickly to his daughter, then again to the other woman, and tried to sit up a bit in his bed. "Megan?" he asked. "What are you doing in New Mexico? I figured you'd be back in L.A. now that they found . . . the body."

She squeezed his hand and let go to pull a tissue from her purse. "I stayed to hear the autopsy report," she replied as she wiped her eyes. She put the tissue in the pocket of her coat. "He was murdered, Captain Divine. I just can't believe it."

Evangeline stepped out of the way to make more room for Megan. She watched with interest to see how the Captain would respond.

He reached up for her hand again, and when she placed it near him, he patted it gently. "I heard this morning. I'm so very sorry," he said, with a voice more gentle than Evangeline thought the Captain capable of. "And you've been here all week?" he asked. "Did you see his body?"

The young woman nodded tearfully.

"I met Miss Flint on Monday," Evangeline announced, speaking from behind the young woman as she tried to join the intimate conversation. "And then we ran into each other again this morning in the morgue."

"What were you doing down in the morgue, Eve?" he asked.

She didn't reply.

"She came to pray for Chaz," Megan answered for her.

Evangeline couldn't tell if the young woman was covering for her or had really believed that was what she was doing there. Whatever the reason for the assistance, she was grateful.

"Anyway, it was terrible," Megan continued. "I had to sneak down there like some criminal." She wiped the tear that had fallen down her cheek. "His wife is here," she added. She seemed to think the Captain would understand. "She was here Monday, too, when I came with Eve and Daniel."

Evangeline peeked around her to see his reaction.

"Oh," he answered. "That must have been ugly."

"She started screaming like a banshee. I was rudely escorted out of the emergency department. It was humiliating." With all the flair of Hollywood, she turned her head away.

"I'm so sorry," the Captain said, patting her hand again.

Evangeline studied the two of them, unsure of which one was the most interesting to observe. Both were giving quite stellar performances, she thought, and she was impressed by how they seemed to play off each other.

"Eve, did you know Megan was a Golden Globe nominee?" he asked, smiling.

"Oh, that was almost three years ago," she said, practicing modesty. "And I didn't win," she added.

"Still, to be nominated is a big deal," he said.

There was a pause as the two grinned at each other.

"Who are you?" Evangeline asked and then was embarrassed to realize that the words had been spoken out loud.

The Captain cleared his throat and dropped the woman's hand. "I think they're going to let me go home this weekend," he said.

"I thought they wanted you to go to a rehab center for a couple of weeks," Evangeline responded.

"I don't need rehab. I survived being shot once and being hit by a drunk driver. I can manage my own rehab." He sat up in the bed.

Evangeline shook her head. "Look, I still think—"

"You were shot?" Megan asked, sounding very impressed.

"It was nothing life-threatening," he answered boastfully. "It's not a terrible scar," he added, and as if it had been scripted, he pulled down his hospital gown to show off the wound on his shoulder that Evangeline had seen a thousand times.

"He was fooling around and got popped at the shooting range," his daughter explained. "A Boy Scout hit him."

"Wow, that looks like it must have been really painful," Megan noted, not paying any attention to what Evangeline had said.

"I winced a little, that's for sure." He glanced down at his scar as if he were reliving the event. He shook his head.

Evangeline wanted to get back to the issue at hand. "Did you tell the doctor you weren't going to rehab?"

Jackson pulled the corner of the gown back over his shoulder and turned to his daughter. "Sure I did," he said. "You've been here long enough. You can go back to Pecos."

Evangeline stepped forward. "That's not what I'm implying."

There was an awkward pause.

Megan cleared her throat. "You know, I just wanted to say hello. I don't need to stay. I can go if you want."

"No, no!" the Captain exclaimed. "You stay!" He smiled. "I want to hear more about what they're saying about Mr. Cheston."

And as if on cue, the door opened and a man's voice bellowed,

"They're saying somebody killed him and then threw him down the hill at the Silver Cross."

All three of them quickly turned in the direction of the announcement and the man who had just entered the room.

"Not that it's any of your business."

FIFTEEN

―━━━━━━━━ ⟨✳✳✳⟩ ━━━━━━━━―

"Hello, Jackson," the uniformed man said and walked over to the bed. "I heard you kicked your last hornet's nest." He grinned.

The visitor was of medium height and build, solid, and was carrying his hat under his arm. Everything on him bore a bright shine—the stars on his collar, the badge on his shirt, the buckle of his belt, the tops of his shoes, the clip on his dark blue tie.

"Lester," the patient addressed him. There wasn't a lot of cheer in his greeting.

The man turned to Evangeline. "Afternoon, Sister," he said with a slight bow. "I know your dad is glad you were able to be here with him. How are things in Pecos? They still making the nuns move out? And have you paid those speeding tickets?"

She managed a smile. "Hello, Chief," she responded. "And things are just fine at the abbey. We're still working with the diocese. And yes, I believe I am all square with the state police." She knew everybody who read the papers was familiar with the monastery's situation, but it seemed to her that everyone in law enforcement knew her history of moving-vehicle violations.

The chief hadn't changed much since the Captain's retirement party. He kept the same hairstyle, the same black mustache. Except for the addition of a few extra pounds around the middle, he looked exactly the same as he did almost fifteen years earlier.

Evangeline had known Les Painter for more than two decades. He had served on the force with her father, but she had never known the Captain to refer to him as a friend. In fact, from the very beginning when Officer Painter had transferred from Albuquerque to Santa Fe, her father had few good things to say about him. The man had risen to the rank of police chief about the time Captain Divine retired. She had always wondered about the coincidence of the shared timing of both.

The visitor then glanced over to Megan, who had shifted to stand closer to the Captain's side. He lifted his eyebrows and held out his hand. "Well, Jackson, you never told me you had such lovely acquaintances."

The young woman took his hand.

"I'm Chief Painter," he announced. "I don't believe I've had the pleasure of being introduced."

Before she could answer, the Captain said, "You don't need to be introduced. What can I do for you, Lester?"

The chief of the Santa Fe Police Department turned his attention away from the young woman. "I was just downstairs speaking to the press, heard you were here and thought I should stop by and check on an old friend." He glanced down the full length of the bed, his eyes stopping for a second at the patient's legs covered by the sheet and blanket, then back up to face Jackson. He started to say something and then seemed to think better of it. He just shook his head as if he felt sorry for the man.

"Well, that's fine of you to drop by." Jackson appeared uncomfortable. He shifted a bit in his bed. "I'll be heading home pretty soon, so things are going very well."

Chief Painter nodded.

There was an awkward pause.

"I'm real glad to hear that. Of course, everybody who knows you knows nothing can keep you down." He sounded sincere. "Even with one leg, you'll probably run circles around everybody else."

Evangeline watched the Captain. She wasn't sure how he was taking the man's comments, and she wondered how long he could stand it before he lost his temper and said some things she knew he had to be thinking.

"So, what are the press and the chief of police doing at the hospital at the same time?" he asked, his words clipped, his tone masking what Eve knew lay just below the surface of the conversation.

The visitor was still grinning.

Jackson waited, feigning ignorance.

"Now, Jack, don't act like you don't know what's happening on your old stomping grounds." He took the hat from under his arm and held it in his hands.

Jackson shrugged. He wasn't giving an inch.

"I'm pretty sure that I recall seeing the first missing person's report and that your name was written somewhere on that file. Am I right about that?"

They all waited for Jackson's reply.

He hesitated, then relented. "I believe I did talk to some of the fine men in blue about a fellow missing in Madrid. It seemed that when the report was sent to your office, there wasn't a lot of interest shown in a county case." He glared at the visitor. "Of course, you know that I am always happy to help out the department. I know how busy things can get for you here in the capital city."

SIXTEEN

"I guess you'll be pretty busy with tracking down the details of what happened." Evangeline tried to sound interested and cheerful. She made her way closer to the bed and stepped between the two men, hoping to keep the Captain from losing his cool.

The chief forced a smile. "Well, we have declared this a homicide investigation, and that does set forth a certain protocol for our department."

"And why exactly is the chief of police in Santa Fe suddenly in charge of a county investigation?" Jackson asked, paying no attention to his daughter's attempt to keep him out of the conversation.

"The sheriff's office doesn't have the kind of financial resources to take this on alone, Jack," Painter replied, moving a little so he could once again see the patient. "Surely you of all people know about that. We work together on the big cases now."

"Especially the ones with television coverage," Jackson muttered.

Megan faced the man standing beside her. "Do you know what happened to Cha—" She stopped herself. "To Mr. Cheston?"

The police chief quickly snapped his attention to the other guest in the room. He seemed to be thinking. "You're the one who hired Jack, isn't that right?" He smiled, watching her. "I do believe that I heard it was a lovely young woman, unrelated to the victim, who had employed a private detective in this case." He paused. "Megan Flint, am I right?"

"I contacted the police first." She seemed uncomfortable with the question, her voice small and tight. "But I was told there needed to be more time for a missing person's report to be filed."

The chief placed his hands on his hips. "Well," he replied with a nod, "we do have procedures in place that we follow." He focused on the Captain. "I'm sure Jack explained all that."

Megan glanced back down at Eve's father. She turned again to the chief. "Of course," she answered. "He was most helpful." She smiled.

"Yes, I'm sure." He winked.

Even as she stood between the two, Evangeline was worried that things would escalate beyond her ability to control.

"But as far as your question about what happened to the victim, unfortunately, we are not at liberty at this time to give any details." His words sounded flat, rehearsed. "But we will be in very close contact with the victim's next of kin." He stopped. "Now, I have that right, don't I, Ms. Flint? You're not related to Mr. Cheston?"

Megan blushed.

"In fact, since we're here together, perhaps you can enlighten me. What was your relationship with the deceased?"

"Chief Painter," Evangeline interrupted. "Perhaps you could do this somewhere other than here in this hospital room."

The chief eyed her and then focused once more on Megan.

"I'm happy to come to the station," Megan volunteered. "I mean, if there are questions that I can answer." She smiled and seemed a bit more self-assured. "I'm staying in town, so I can come any time."

Chief Painter appeared to be thinking about Evangeline's request and Megan's offer. He narrowed his eyes at the young woman. "As long as we have a contact number for you, it's fine that we finish this discussion later."

"Perfect," Evangeline responded, gently patting the chief on the shoulder.

"Okay, then," Chief Painter said, reading the signs. "I'm glad to see you're doing well, Jackson."

There was no response from the Captain.

"Ladies," Painter added with a nod and headed out the door.

Evangeline interrupted before the Captain could call out the expletive that she knew he was thinking.

"So . . ." she said cheerfully, "now that you've had the chance to meet the chief of police for the city of Santa Fe, Megan, why don't you pull up that chair by the window and have a seat?"

SEVENTEEN

"What exactly did you tell them?" John Ewing stood in the door-way of the small, cluttered office at the stables. He had just returned from his day's excursion and was surprised to find the police, the news vans, and at least a dozen bystanders gathered near the gate to his property at the Silver Cross. He had learned about the body as soon as he pulled into the driveway. He managed to park, but an officer met him before he was even able to get out of his truck. The interview that followed with the policeman in the house had lasted almost an hour. After that, he had to talk to the customers who had been the two other witnesses. This was the first time he'd been able to be alone with his employee.

Aaron shrugged. He was hanging up the saddles, wiping them down after their use in the day's ride. "I told them exactly what we saw," he answered.

"And what was that?"

"That we were up on the top, at the end of the trail. I was

showing them the view before we headed back. And then the woman saw it," he explained.

Aaron knew his boss had already heard an earful from the two customers. They, too, had been questioned by the police, and even though they had been excused, they had chosen to wait for the proprietor of the stables to return. He'd heard that Mr. Ewing had already been informed that he was paying the medical costs for the woman's ambulance ride to the clinic just three miles from town, where she was checked out and released, as well as the dry cleaning costs for the damage done to her brand-new jeans. It turned out that would be more than the doctor's bill. She had been walking around the ranch, making sure everyone saw what a mess she had fallen into.

"It was on the west side of the wash, where the snow was melting." He waited. Apparently, that was not enough of an answer.

"The woman saw the body first. She screamed, her boyfriend or husband, whoever he was, fell off Lucy, spooked the mare terrible, then the woman fainted and she fell backward into the . . ." He hesitated. "Well, you saw how that ended." He was trying not to grin. "Or at the very least, you smelled it."

"And then?" Ewing asked, not amused.

Aaron took a rag and wiped off the stirrups. He also had already answered the questions asked by numerous police officers, signed a statement, and excused himself from the reporters trying to get an exclusive.

"Clover and I walked their horses back here. I drove the four-wheeler to pick them up, brought them to the stables, called the sheriff and the ambulance, because she was crying that she'd hurt her neck. When the ambulance arrived, I rode down there to see if I could tell who it was."

"And could you?" The rancher filled up the space in the doorway. He stood firm, both arms leaning on the frame.

"He had on leather loafers, no socks, a light jacket. I don't think he had been hiking." He shook his head. "I brushed the snow away from his face." He turned to his employer. "I don't think the police were real happy about that, but I told them I was just making sure I couldn't save him. How was I to know for sure that he was dead?" He waited.

Ewing was waiting as well.

"It was him."

John Ewing blew out a breath and turned, keeping his back to the cowboy. "They find out what killed him?" Ewing's voice sounded far away.

"I couldn't see nothing once they pulled him out of the snow," Aaron replied. "They put up a big tarp around the body while they dug him out. Jerilyn was on the ambulance that came to get that woman, and you know how big her mouth is. By the time the state police were here, it looked like the Placer gold rush. They must have closed down all of Cerrillos and Madrid. Anyway, I couldn't see anything after that. And they weren't talking." The young man paused. He was surprised by all the questions. "You worried this will hurt the business?"

Ewing spun around. "I couldn't care less about the business," he blurted out.

The two men didn't speak. They listened as the helicopter came closer and could hear the vehicles still driving past the stables, the drivers and passengers hoping for a better view and the voices of folks walking by the property.

Aaron finally broke the silence. "Does Mr. Biltmore know?"

The rancher didn't answer at first.

Aaron waited and then turned back and continued cleaning the saddles. He could see that his boss was upset, and after hearing no response for so long, figured their conversation was finished. He knew when to quit prying.

"Mr. Biltmore left the country a week ago."

Aaron faced Ewing.

"He was upset about something but wouldn't tell me what." The older man pulled out a handkerchief from his back pocket and wiped his forehead. It was not warm outside, but John Ewing had certainly been sweating.

"You tell the police anything else?" Ewing wanted to know.

Aaron dug his hands into his pockets and shook his head. "I don't know anything else to tell," he said, lifting his eyes to get a look at the other man.

The rancher watched him for a second, turned away, and nodded. "No, I guess you don't," was all he said.

EIGHTEEN

"This was never anything you and I discussed." Captain Divine was sitting in his wheelchair in the family conference room on the third floor. His discharge was scheduled for later that day, and he and several hospital personnel, along with Evangeline, were gathered to discuss his continued care at home.

Evangeline had spent the night in Madrid, getting settled back into her old room, buying necessary groceries, and trying to make the arrangements needed for the patient to return home. She had gone out to dinner with Megan, learned more about the young movie star and how she had been taking care of her mother after she suffered a stroke. Megan enjoyed being an actress, but it wasn't just about the fame. She needed the money to pay for her mother's care. Evangeline had even learned more about the young woman's relationship with the Hollywood director. She had planned to share what she'd learned with the Captain. She was told about the team meeting concerning his discharge when she arrived at the hospital.

"Mr. Divine," the social worker started.

"It's pronounced *Diveen*," the Captain interrupted.

"Mr. Divine," she started again, pronouncing the name correctly and trying to ease the tension between the patient and his daughter. It was clear to everyone gathered that he was hearing for the first time that Evangeline was planning to go back to Madrid and care for him. "Since you have declined rehabilitation services at a local facility, we are willing to extend our home care to you." She tapped her pen on the papers in front of her. "But we are not able to be with you twenty-four hours a day." She leaned back in her seat. "And it is the consensus of everyone around this table, along with your doctors, that you cannot stay by yourself."

He folded his arms across his chest. "And how does everyone around this table, along with my doctors," he sneered, "know exactly what I can and cannot do?"

"Are you able to transfer from your chair to the toilet?" the charge nurse asked. She waited.

There was no response.

"Can you get into and out of the shower without assistance?" She clasped her hands. "Is your house even wheelchair accessible?" She took a breath.

He did not answer.

"Captain Divine," the nurse said with respect, "this is a major life transition for you. You have shown great commitment to your recovery while you've been in the hospital, and you've done excellent work with the physical and occupational therapists. Your residual limb is in great shape, the wound is healed, and the swelling continues to decrease. You should be able to be fitted for the prosthetic in a few more weeks." She paused. "But you are not ready to manage all of this at home by yourself."

Captain Divine still didn't speak.

The social worker looked over the discharge orders from the doctor. "We will send a physical therapist to Madrid three times a week. The nurse will come once, and we can order a nurse tech to come every other morning of the week to assist you with your shower and dress. Your insurance will cover all of those services for about two months. After that we can reassess and continue home care if needed." She glanced up at the patient.

He was staring at Eve. "When did you make these arrangements?"

She had been listening to the social worker and didn't realize at first that he was speaking to her. "I'm hearing about this for the first time just like you," she replied.

"You know what I mean," he said. "When did you have this conversation with your superiors at Pecos and decide that you were going home with me?"

She glanced away, unsure of how to answer. She had, after all, known this was going to happen the day after the surgery. Brother Oliver had told her to take all the time she needed, but she had asked for only a couple of months. She wanted to get back to the convent before the building project began. She still had hope that she could change the minds of those wishing to separate the monks from the nuns and move the women to another area of the campus. She wanted another meeting with her superiors.

"Eve," he called out, "when did you make this decision?"

She shook her head. She didn't want to do this in front of the others at the table. She had planned this conversation with her father as one without witnesses but had not taken the time to have it before the nurse asked for a family conference. She knew it was now or never. She took a breath and plunged in.

NINETEEN

---✦※✦---

"I asked for the leave of absence a day after your surgery," she began. "I had a meeting with the vice superior, and he agreed it was the right thing to do."

"You and Dorisanne . . ." He lifted his chin when he said his other daughter's name. "The two of you also make this same agreement?"

Evangeline shifted in her chair. The other women around the table fidgeted, seeming to feel her discomfort.

"And everybody else here, they knew too? You told these strangers before you told me?" he asked.

"You're accusing *me* of talking to strangers before family about your health?" She stopped, realizing it would do no good to get into an argument about how she found out about the surgery in the first place. She took in a breath and began again.

"Dorisanne and I decided that I would take the leave of absence and help you get adjusted at home. I think a couple of months will do it. I didn't need to ask your permission to leave the order to provide your care. And yes, I discussed with the nurses here the other options when you stubbornly refused to go to the rehab center." She could feel the anger rising in her throat, her jaw tightening. She decided she had said enough.

There was a long, awkward pause and then someone's pager went off. The social worker reached down to her belt and silenced the noise. The vibrations echoed softly in the quiet room.

The Captain slumped a bit, resting his elbows on the arms of the wheelchair. He seemed to calm down. "So, this is how it all begins?" he asked.

No one responded.

"First the children have a conversation and make decisions for you, then your daughter decides to leave her home, her vocation of twenty years, and move back in, and then strangers barely old enough to vote tell you whether or not you're strong enough to get out of a chair by yourself." He stopped and glanced over at Eve, who had closed her eyes.

He waited. "You lose your leg, and then you lose your right to make decisions for yourself."

"Mr. Divine, I don't think that's what is happening here," the nurse explained.

"Oh, you don't?" he asked, spinning around to face her.

The charge nurse glanced around the table. "Adult children want to show the love they feel for their parents. They do that by making sure their parents are cared for when they are sick, when they need medical attention. Sometimes children are able to manage that care themselves, and sometimes they make arrangements for professionals to provide the care. Conversations have to take place about those decisions regarding care, and sometimes those conversations don't include the parent. The children make the best decisions they can to care for their parents because they love their parents. And that is what love does."

No one seemed to know what to say after such an impassioned speech. The social worker tapped her pen nervously. The physical therapist reached for her cup of coffee and took a sip. Evangeline watched her father, waiting for him to lash out.

A few minutes passed, and the vibrating noise from the social worker's pager sounded again. She silenced it.

There was a long and awkward pause before the Captain spoke.

"You'll stay two months and then you'll go back." It was more of a command than a request.

"Yes," Eve responded. "I only have leave for two months."

"Then two months it is," he said.

TWENTY

"Anybody home?" The screen door slammed as Daniel walked into the house.

"We're back here," was the reply.

Evangeline entered the front room. "Well, what a wonderful surprise," she said. She hugged him, then felt the shove against her legs and glanced down. "Trooper!" she sang out and knelt down to welcome her father's dog back home.

The big yellow Labrador circled around a number of times, her tail almost knocking Evangeline down.

"I know somebody who'll be happy to see you." She stood up. "Go find the Captain," she said.

Trooper bounded for the back bedroom. A shout of excitement followed.

Evangeline smiled. "Well, I guess there's at least one girl he's happy to have back here." She stepped away from the door. "Here, let me take your coat." She held out her hands while Daniel removed his outerwear. "Have a seat," she said and went to hang up Daniel's jacket.

"What time did you get home?" Daniel asked, taking his place on the sofa.

"It was about eight last night," she answered, sitting down across from him. "It took forever for the doctor to come around and sign the papers." She pulled her legs up, tucking her feet under her. "We waited six hours." She motioned to the back of the house with her thumb. "He was fit to be tied."

Daniel laughed. "I guess that's one nursing unit that's glad the insurance company can limit a patient's stay in the hospital."

"I suspect you're right." She tugged at her socks. "And here I thought they were being so attentive to his medical needs. The truth is they were just trying to get him well enough to discharge him."

"I can hear you." The Captain rolled into the room in his wheelchair. Trooper rested in his lap.

"I don't think that's how it's supposed to work with a service animal," Daniel noted as Jackson stopped beside the sofa. The dog sat up, obscuring the Captain's view.

He made a clicking noise and Trooper climbed down gently, as if she had been given exact instructions on how to exit without causing harm. She went into the kitchen to get some water.

"Yeah, well, we'll work on it," he replied.

"So how was it to sleep in your own bed last night?" Daniel asked.

"It was good," he lied. The truth was that neither he nor Evangeline had slept well.

"Nothing like your own bed, right?" his friend noted.

"That's for sure." He glanced over at Eve, and she got the message not to add anything more.

"Tell me, what's the latest on our Hollywood victim?" Jackson said.

Daniel smiled. "I wondered how long it would take you to get back to business."

He stretched out and crossed his legs at his ankles. "Well, it doesn't appear that the cause of death was a fall from the hiking trail."

"Yeah, we knew that. It would have taken a running dive to get that far. Besides, the chief gave me that much information."

Daniel nodded. "His toxicology report was probably the most interesting."

Evangeline had leaned in. "Was it crank?" she asked.

Daniel glanced over at Eve. "How do you know about meth?"

"I know some things," she replied.

The Captain rolled his eyes. "She's gotten tight with Megan," he noted. "The poor girl thought she was making a confession when really Eve was pumping her for information."

"You and Megan are close?" Daniel asked.

"I wouldn't call us close," Eve answered. "And she did not think she was making a confession. Chaz has a history of addiction. Megan said he had stopped doing crack and hashish but recently had gotten hooked on crystal meth, ice, crank. He liked the quick energy boost, claimed it helped him write the scripts better."

"Chaz?" Daniel asked, sounding surprised to hear the nun calling the dead man by his nickname.

"Can you believe her?" Jackson pointed his thumb over at his daughter. "A week and a half out of the convent and she's talking like somebody from the vice squad."

Daniel laughed. "Well, it wasn't crack or hashish or crank that was found in his bloodstream," he responded. "It was etorphine hydrochloride."

"M99?" Eve could see the surprise in both men's eyes. "What?"

"How do you know about M99?" Daniel asked.

"*Dexter* on Showtime," she answered.

The two men looked at each other.

"You said you hadn't seen a movie in ten years," Daniel said. "You don't even know what Denzel Washington looks like."

"Six years," she corrected him. "But I had a whole week and a half to watch television at the hospital." She shrugged. "Megan had a small part on one of the episodes of *Dexter*, and she told me where to find the reruns."

The two men appeared to be waiting for more of an explanation.

"Dexter is a vigilante and a serial killer. He likes to drug his victims with etorphine hydrochloride because it renders them paralyzed."

"M99?" the Captain repeated, rolling his eyes at Eve.

Daniel nodded. "Well, apparently, it's also a good drug for whatever the murderer of our victim liked to do. It looks like it was a shot right to the heart, a dart gun most likely."

"A dart gun?" Eve questioned, trying not to sound too excited.

TWENTY-ONE

"Well, what do you think about that news?" Evangeline was helping the Captain into bed.

It was early for sleep, eight o'clock at night, but neither father nor daughter had been able to take the afternoon naps they were hoping to enjoy his first full day home because of all the company. After Daniel left, the home health nurse showed up, followed by one of the neighbors who brought green chile stew and stayed for a visit, and then the phone rang most of the afternoon with well-wishes from folks in the community before another of Jackson's friends from the police department dropped by to welcome him home. It had been a very busy day, and both Evangeline and Jackson were exhausted.

"What?" the Captain asked. "What news? Delphine buying a new car?" He was recalling his neighbor's delight when she dropped off the stew and showed them her purchase. She had just bought a new Toyota Camry that she'd found on the Internet.

"No, not Delphine's new car, which, now that you mention it, did I tell you about the weird smell inside?" Evangeline pulled the covers over him.

He shook his head. "No," he answered. "The phone rang while you were outside getting a closer look. I talked to Donnie for about half an hour, and then you left to pick up the mail."

She nodded. "Oh, that's right." She glanced around the room. "Do you want another blanket?" She didn't see one but figured she could find more bed linens in the hall closet.

"No, this is enough."

Evangeline studied the bed. "Okay, you look like you're in there good. Do you want another pillow? That one comfortable?"

"It's fine," he replied. "So, what about the smell?"

She seemed confused. "Oh, yeah. It smelled like rotten eggs or something. Delphine didn't seem to notice. She just kept showing off all the controls and buttons. But it really stunk inside."

Jackson laughed. "Delphine hasn't been able to smell since she fainted and hit her head in the bathroom."

"Really?" Evangeline hadn't heard that bit of information about her neighbor.

"A year or so ago," he responded. "She had food poisoning, and passed out after running to the toilet for the hundredth time." He paused. "Or at least that's how she tells it."

Evangeline made a sort of humming noise. "Well then, I guess it was a perfect arrangement. She gets a great buy and somebody gets a smelly car off their hands." She grinned. "She won't have many passengers, though, that's for sure."

"Nobody will ride with her anyway. Delphine drives like a nun."

Evangeline seemed surprised by the dig. "I beg your pardon."

"You're a good driver when you obey the speed limit . . ." He stopped to give her a look. "I've seen some of those other sisters from Pecos driving in Santa Fe. They go twenty miles an hour, switch lanes without checking their mirrors or signaling. And they can't park square in a lot marked with lanes big enough for trucks with haulers. You know what I'm talking about. They just think God will take care of them." He slid down a bit in the bed, reached up, and fluffed his pillow.

Evangeline shrugged. "Most of the sisters really are terrible drivers."

"I know I'm right," he noted smugly.

"Well, anyway, I'm not talking about Delphine's new car. I'm talking about the toxicology findings that Daniel told us about this morning." She sat down in the rocking chair across from the bed. "Etorphine hydrochloride in his system, who would have guessed that?"

Captain Divine watched his daughter. He didn't respond.

"So who do you think killed him?" She started rocking. "I know his wife wasn't too happy with Mr. Hollywood Playboy. His son may have had something to lose if there was a divorce. There's the producer that Megan told me about who had been monitoring Cheston closely since his rehab stint. He seemed to have been mad at the director because some of the money earmarked for the next movie was unaccounted for. There's his drug buddies, whoever they are, and there's this mystery guy who lives out at Cedar Hill that I heard some police officers at the hospital talking about who apparently was a known associate." She folded her arms across her chest, pondering all the possible suspects.

"There's also Megan," the Captain added.

Evangeline stopped rocking. "Why would she want him killed?" she asked. "Wasn't she the one who hired you to try and find him?"

"Good cover, don't you think?" He waited.

Eve considered the suggestion.

She was preparing to start her defense of the young woman when he interrupted.

"Eve, what are you doing?"

She shrugged, not understanding the question. "I'm sitting here, talking to you, feeling pretty confident that Megan has not killed her boyfriend."

"No." He shook his head. "I know you love a lost cause, but you're way too invested in Megan's alibi. You almost fell off the sofa when Daniel mentioned this report. I heard you asking the nurse about the drugs Cheston is accused of taking. Why aren't you reading your prayer books and going to your room for silent meditation? Why aren't you making arrangements to go to the church in town or even back to Pecos for daily services?"

She wouldn't meet his stare. "I pray," she answered.

He kept watching her. "You know what I mean," he said knowingly.

"No," she replied. "I don't know what you mean. I'm on a leave of absence," she explained. "I'm talking to you about something I thought interested you."

She got up. "I guess I was wrong." She walked over and tucked in the covers a bit. "I'll get your pain pill and then you can go to sleep." And she turned to walk out of the room before he could stop her.

TWENTY-TWO

On the front porch of the house off Highway 14, the one across a canyon and down a dirt road that twisted and turned through mined hills and clumps of juniper bushes, Evangeline sat, watching the stars, the glow of the late winter's full moon. It was as quiet around the house of her childhood as it was at the monastery, where she often walked late at night, down along the Pecos River or up on the trails of the mountain. Part of the reason her transition to the religious order was not as difficult as it had been for some of the other monks and nuns was because she lived in a community that was exactly like the place where she had grown up.

She loved the Sangre de Cristo Mountains. She loved the smell of piñon wood burning in a small, outdoor pit. She loved the barrenness of the desert, the austerity of the landscape, the life that struggled and survived there. She knew that if she joined a cloistered life there in New Mexico, at the monastery in Pecos only fifty miles or so from Madrid, she would have all the time and space and opportunity she wanted to be in and with and on this land to which she was so deeply and intimately connected.

The work of the Benedictines was important. She honored the daily schedule of prayer and worship and work. She was committed to community life and did the best she knew how to live in communal relationship with the other monks and nuns. She gave her heart to Christ and herself in service to others. She was also hopeful that being a monastic would help her with her weaknesses, tame her temper, and keep her willful spirit at bay. She did not, after all, want to turn into her father.

But if pushed, Evangeline would tell the truth. She was a nun in Pecos because she loved the desert. She was in love with the land. She could not separate at all her devotion to the desert from her devotion to her faith and to her call to service. She pulled the blanket she had brought from inside the house over her shoulders and leaned back against the steps of the porch, gazing into the velvet night.

She had not answered the Captain. She pretended not to have time to talk and busied herself with locating his medicines, preparing him for sleep, organizing phone messages and mail accumulated during his recent hospital stay. He had tried to bring the topic up again when she brought in the evening's pain pill, but she had refused to engage, refused to reply to his query, and had simply informed him that they both needed sleep. And with that announcement she had ended his questions, turned out the light, and closed his door. She had not allowed for more of the conversation that she knew she would eventually have to have with someone, sometime.

Just not now, she thought, shaking away the thoughts of how easy it was to pack and leave Pecos, how uncomplicated it had been for her to ask for the leave of absence, how little she had missed her life at the monastery since having been away. She would face these signs later. *But for tonight*, she told herself, *I will ponder the stars and the tides of the moon, and this small familiar place where I sit.*

She decided she would not think about what it all meant, being away from the monastery, being away from the observed hours of the day, the liturgy, and the community and the constant sense that she could never quite get it right. She would not think about how restless she had felt for the last few months, how dissatisfied she had felt with the life she'd chosen. She would not consider how often she got in trouble for questioning authority or trying to raise consciousness among the other nuns about social causes. She would not think about how Brother Oliver rolled his eyes when she asked about keeping another stray dog, buying extra milk for the cats that wandered on the property. She would not focus on the trouble she got into when she talked to a reporter about the new rule that meant pushing out the nuns and making them leave the monastery proper.

For now, she thought, *I will not think about why I feel so alive hearing news of drugs and motives for homicide or why this young starlet has my attention and why I feel so driven to help her. I will not worry about the passion that has been ignited within me.*

"You always fought for the underdog," Daniel had reminded her that morning. Maybe that was all this was. Maybe it had just been a long time since she'd been pulled in to a fight for someone with all the odds stacked up against her. Maybe that pull had given her a dose of excitement she hadn't felt at the monastery. Maybe it was just the break she needed and it wouldn't last long, and then she would be able to go back to the life she had.

For now, however, she wouldn't think any more of her emotions, her ambivalence, or the Captain's questions. For now she would just rest. And with that thought she drifted off, without ever noticing the lone hiker standing on the hill above her, watching her as she started to doze, and finally walking away just after Eve finally dropped off to sleep.

TWENTY-THREE

――――――※※※――――――

It was exactly three weeks from the day of the Captain's surgery when Megan Flint made the call from Los Angeles, breaking the news that she had been deemed a "person of interest" in the murder of her boyfriend, Charles Cheston. Jackson Divine had just returned home from his first appointment with the prosthetist to be fitted for his new artificial leg, and he was tired from the long trip to and from Albuquerque. Evangeline was making lunch for them both when the phone rang.

The Captain spoke to Megan first. He listened to her concerns, had her recite the questions she'd been asked by the detectives, the specific reasons she thought they were interested in her, and exactly what she had told them. But then when asked for his advice, his help, he had simply suggested that she find a good attorney. He was sympathetic to her plight but made no offer of assistance before handing the phone to Evangeline.

She took the call, having been able to make out most of what had been said in the conversation and surprised by her father's response. After she exchanged greetings with Megan, she also listened, offering words of encouragement, comfort, and ultimately an invitation to drive out to Madrid to see them both as soon as she returned to New Mexico.

When she walked over to put the cordless phone back in its cradle, Evangeline considered the Captain's lack of interest in Megan's announcement, noticed his slumped position in his wheelchair, and was aware of the silence that had begun on the trip back from his appointment. Without immediate comment, she headed back into the kitchen, finished making lunch, placed the sandwiches and chips on plates, put the plates on the table, and informed Jackson that lunch was served. The Captain slowly wheeled himself from the sitting room over to his place at the table. He waited as Evangeline bowed her head and prayed.

She reached for her lunch and started to eat. It was quiet for a few minutes as she considered how to start a conversation.

"Your sandwich okay?" she asked.

He nodded. "You get rid of that cat?"

A stray cat had shown up at the detective agency office and Evangeline was feeding it. The Captain had told her to call animal control. It was the same conversation he'd had with her for most of her life regarding the animals she kept taking in.

"She's fine," Eve replied. "She just comes for morning milk and then she's off for her day. She's not a bother, and no, I didn't call animal control. Instead I took her to the vet, got her vaccinated, and found out she was already fixed."

He grunted in response.

"I even named her." She waited but he didn't ask.

"Daisy," she said. "Because she's yellow," she added.

The Captain rolled his eyes.

"Dr. Rogers seems nice," she noted, referring to the doctor who was in charge of the prosthetics company. "I think he'll take good care of you."

The Captain did not respond. He just kept chewing his food.

"I guess your leg will be sore for a few months," she said. "Especially when the prosthetic gets fitted and set."

She glanced up at her father.

He simply nodded again.

"Well, what do you think of him?" she asked, trying again to engage him.

"He seems like a decent salesman," he replied, picking up a few chips. "Is there any milk?"

Evangeline got up and poured them both a glass of milk. She walked back to the table, placing one of the glasses in front of her father, the other by her plate. He seemed to be studying it.

"Is something wrong?" she asked.

He glanced up. "It's funny, don't you think?"

"What's funny?" she asked, taking her seat.

"How simple things are when you've got all your body parts." He took a swallow of the milk. "How easy it was for you to get up, walk to the refrigerator, reach up in the cabinet for glasses, pour the drinks, walk back, sit down." He wiped his mouth. "You know how much thought it would have taken me to figure out those simple movements?"

Evangeline lowered her eyes and took another bite of her sandwich.

"First of all, you would have had to move from your place at the table because I can't get past you into the kitchen. I couldn't even reach the glasses in that cabinet. Once I managed to pour the milk, I couldn't carry both of the cups in here while pushing myself in this wheelchair." He shook his head. "Even one cup of milk would probably have spilled all over me. Everything requires planning now." He pushed his plate away from him.

"Yes, but that's the good thing about the prosthetic," Evangeline said, trying to encourage her father. "With your new leg, it'll feel more normal."

"More normal?" he asked mockingly. "I have no right foot," he added. "I'll be wearing a plastic leg that rubs my skin raw. I have to learn to walk again. Do you know the percentage of men my age who actually end up making use of their prosthetics, actually end up getting up and staying out of the wheelchair?"

Evangeline shook her head. She hadn't heard the statistic.

"Twenty percent," he told her. "Only twenty percent of men over the age of sixty-five actually end up using their fake legs. Most of them just can't do it. It's too much work; and besides, they know that it doesn't matter anyway."

"They know *what* doesn't matter?" she asked.

The Captain's eyes met his daughter's. "They know learning to walk again, learning to adjust to a plastic body part, doesn't matter because losing a foot is just the beginning. In a couple of years, it will be the other foot, and then there will be an infection in the upper leg, and they'll cut more off of both limbs. And what senior amputee do you know who can get around without both legs?" He waited for only a second. "None," he answered for himself. "At my age, you just can't overcome the odds."

Evangeline waited. She finished her sandwich and drank some milk. "First of all, I don't know where you got that information about twenty percent of older men not using their prosthetics. I read the same brochures you did, and I never saw that statistic. And second, when did you ever think of yourself as being like men your own age? You're Captain Jackson Divine. You've never walked away from a challenge."

"Well, I'm likely not to walk away from this one, either. It will be more like rolling away from it."

And just like that, the light came on. "So that's it. You think you'll never walk again so that's the reason you won't help Megan." She shook her head. "Boy, you are not the man I thought you were."

"I gave her good advice," he said.

"What is that supposed to mean?"

"The police are just trying to scare her out of some information. They don't have anything on her to connect her to the victim's death."

"How do you know that?" She got up from the table. "How do you know what they have or don't have? Have you talked to Daniel?"

He shook his head. "Not since he came by a few days ago."

"Why did you tell her to get a lawyer?" Evangeline was curious.

"I'd tell you to get a lawyer if the police wanted to question you."

"Do you think police officers ask unfair questions or don't tell the truth about the nature of their interviews?"

The Captain smiled. "I think that police officers are the most honorable men and women I know."

Evangeline waited. "But?"

"But police officers like to close their cases. They like things to fit nicely in whatever box they have made for the crime." He rested his hands on the wheels of the chair. "And if they think they have a suspect, they'll do whatever they can to get the evidence they need."

"Even participate in trickery or dubious interviews?"

"I just think a lawyer helps level the playing field."

"Why didn't you offer to help her? You know the playing field pretty well. And if what you say is true and they've decided that she's the suspect who best fits in the box, then she'll need some help handling their questions."

He shook his head and pushed himself away from the table, then turned his chair and pointed it in the direction of the back of the house. "I'm an old man with only one good leg. I'm pretty sure my days of leveling playing fields are done. She'll find a good lawyer and get out of this."

And he wheeled himself away before his daughter could say anything more.

TWENTY-FOUR

"He's been in bed the whole day." Evangeline had taken the phone outside. She was sitting in the rocker on the porch talking to her sister. "I thought he was doing fine after the surgery, but it was like something happened to him yesterday when he went to get fitted for the prosthetic."

"Did it not fit?" Dorisanne asked.

"What?"

"Is he depressed because the leg doesn't fit?"

"He hasn't suddenly gained weight and can't fit into his prom dress, Dorisanne. He's lost his foot, part of his leg. He has to have help to go to the bathroom. You know how hard this is for him?"

"He lets you help him go to the bathroom?"

Evangeline didn't respond. She blew out a breath and kept rocking. "Are you coming to see him?" she asked.

"I already came," Dorisanne replied.

Evangeline stopped rocking. "What? When?" She knew she had been with their father every day since the surgery.

"I was there when you came home from the hospital. I stayed with Michael and Sarah."

There was a long pause as Evangeline tried to take in the news that her sister had been in Madrid, staying with friends who lived only a couple of miles from their parents' house, and she had not come home.

"I saw you fall asleep on the porch that second night."

Evangeline did not respond but remembered the evening she'd dozed off and slept outside all night.

"I got a rental car at the airport. I drove to the hospital, but you had already left. I just didn't feel like I should show up at the house his first night home. I stayed with Michael and Sarah, and then the next day I watched all the cars come and go from the house. That night I saw you sleeping outside. I just couldn't come over there, Eve."

Still no response from the other end.

"Besides, I only had two days off. I had to be at work," she explained.

Still nothing.

"I'm coming back in a few weeks. Did you get my messages? Did he get the card?"

Evangeline shook her head. She was having a difficult time digesting the news.

"Look, the last time I was in Madrid, we got in a horrible fight," Dorisanne confessed. "I said some things; he said some things. It was real hurtful, and I just don't feel ready to see him again."

Evangeline remained silent.

"It doesn't matter. You don't want to hear any of this stuff."

"Why wouldn't I want to hear about what happened between the two of you?"

"Oh, Eve. You're a nun. You married God."

"What is that supposed to mean?"

"Nothing," came the reply.

"No, really, Dorisanne, what do you mean by saying that I don't get to know about the family news because I'm a nun?"

A long breath poured through the phone.

"Ever since you joined the monastery, I just feel like you can't be bothered with family stuff."

"What?" Eve sat straight up in the chair. "How can you say that? I was here when Mama died. I was here when arrangements were made for her funeral. I visited as often as I could. I've been here for birthdays and your wedding. I've listened to your hard-luck stories about Vegas. I was here for the Captain's retirement party. What have I missed by being a nun?"

"You've missed all the mess, Eve. Sure, you show up for the death and the funeral, the parties, the planned events. But you missed holding the bucket when Mama vomited three times a day for a month. You missed having to apologize over and over for the Captain's rants at the nurses and doctors while she was sick. You missed his drinking binges and having to go pick him up from the Mineshaft at two in the morning. You missed the creditors calling when he didn't pay the bills. You missed planning my wedding with me and Mama. You missed sitting with us in the hospital waiting room and hearing the surgeon tell us they didn't get all the cancer. You missed hearing that Robbie was beat up for not paying off a loan shark. I cannot name all that you missed in the twenty years you've been living at that monastery."

Evangeline sank back down. She'd never known Dorisanne felt like this.

"I'm sorry, Eve. It's not really like all that. You were there when you needed to be there. Mama knew you were there and I was glad to take care of her. I wanted to take care of her. Look, I'm sorry I stayed with Michael and Sarah and didn't come. I'll be back in a few weeks."

There was no reply.

"Eve?"

"Yeah, I'm still here."

"I'm sorry, okay?"

And the only thing she could do was nod and end the call.

TWENTY-FIVE

Three days after the phone call with her sister, and three weeks after her father's surgery and her temporary departure from the monastery, Evangeline was lonesome for her mother. *She's the only one*, she thought, *who could really help me deal with Dorisanne, make peace with her, and understand the truth of what she said.* And she was the only one who could help Eve figure out what to do with the Captain and his recent spiral downward.

Since it was Saturday, Evangeline decided to attend Mass at the local parish. The Captain declined her invitation to join her. So after she fixed his breakfast, carried it to him in bed, and cleaned up the dishes, she headed into town in the Captain's truck.

Father Steve was new to the little parish in Madrid. He was young and inexperienced in pastoral ministry, but Evangeline liked the young man and appreciated his sermon and the ways in which he cared for the little community. She knew he pastored four other churches and that he was on the road traveling from parish to parish more than he was actually in the pulpit, but he seemed comfortable with the arrangements of his assignment and cheerful during the Saturday morning Mass at the Madrid church.

After the service she introduced herself to him, noting her vocation and her recent leave of absence to take care of the Captain. Father Steve smiled knowingly when she mentioned her family name, and in good pastoral fashion asked about Jackson's condition and if there was anything he could do as the pastor to the family. He explained that he was available if she thought the Captain wanted him to stop by and offer a blessing for the sick or an anointing for his healing.

"No," Evangeline had said. "I think he would only see your visit as being pushed upon you both by me."

And with that the priest had nodded and given his farewell greetings, needing to leave so that he could make it to the noon service in Galisteo. As he drove away, Evangeline turned and walked to the back of the church and into the cemetery where her mother was buried. She brushed off the tombstone, picked up a few limbs and leaves from the grave, and then kissed her fingers and touched the top of the stone before she sat down and leaned against it.

It was a beautiful spring day, bright sun, perfectly blue sky. Evangeline took in a deep breath and closed her eyes. She thought about her mother, the gentle way she cared for her daughters, the fierce way she loved her family. Evangeline remembered her easy laugh and the ways she could always bring the Captain down from his rants and raves, how she always seemed to be able to soothe his troubled waters.

"I love you, Mama," she said. "And I miss you so much." She

slid her feet beneath her. "I wish you were here to tell me what to do about the Captain. I'm really worried," she added. "He just doesn't seem to be coming out of this funk."

Evangeline opened her eyes and watched as the pigeons flew in and out of the church belfry. She could see the cars snaking in and around the town, the tourists coming and going along the Turquoise Trail. She could hear the traffic noise and the breeze dancing through the dry cottonwood leaves scattered around the cemetery. She thought about her mom and the things she would say when Jackson was angry, when the two girls would complain to her about his temper or his strict means of discipline with them.

"He's a lion," she once told them. "He thinks he has to roar to make his voice heard. He thinks being loud and strong is what a father is supposed to do."

Eve had rolled her eyes. "He's not a lion, he's a big, mean bully."

Mother pulled Eve into her arms, holding her tight, pressing her lips into the back of the young girl's neck. "He loves you," she had said. "He just wants you to be safe. That's what he cares about most." Dorisanne squeezed in, trying to get close to their mother. "You're just like him, Eve," she said.

"Is that true? Am I a lion too? Am I going to be a bully like him?"

"You're not a bully," her mother said. "You're strong, but that doesn't make you mean."

And even with the reassurance, Evangeline grew up always worried that her strength would be her downfall.

Their mother had always been the peacemaker in their home. She had been the calm presence and the keeper of love and light in their family. And now that she was gone, Evangeline wasn't sure that any of the three of them who remained knew how to bring about the peace they all needed. Especially the Captain. Especially now.

Evangeline remembered something else. She knew that her mother had been worried about the Captain's decision to retire and leave the force, and even though she did not know all of the facts about his choice, she knew that it wasn't only because he wanted to start his own detective agency. Neither of her parents would explain what happened in Santa Fe and why he was retiring before the age of sixty-five, but she knew it wasn't simply a decision based on his desire to run his own business. Something had happened. Evangeline just didn't know what.

One afternoon after the Captain's surprise announcement, her mother had driven over to the monastery and surprised Evangeline with a visit. They had taken a walk. "The man has to work," Evangeline recalled her mother saying as they hiked the dusty path. "Your father, I just don't know if he'll have enough to do as a private detective. He lives for his work. The only thing that really gets him out of bed most mornings is that need to solve a mystery or order someone else's chaos. If this idea of his doesn't pan out, I just don't know how he'll survive."

"He lives for his work," Eve repeated to herself and then stood up and brushed herself off.

"Thanks, Mom," she said as she turned and touched the head-stone once more. "A murdered Hollywood director may be just the chaos he needs right now."

TWENTY-SIX

—— ⊹✳⊹ ——

"Megan's here," Evangeline announced when she saw the limousine pull into their driveway.

The Captain was in his room, back in bed after Eve had made him get up and go to the table for his breakfast. After her revelation at her mother's grave, Evangeline hoped that his former client would give him reason to get up and stay up that morning. Prior to her epiphany at the cemetery, she had tried everything from phone calls from his old colleagues to rented movies from the video store to special sugar-free desserts purchased from his favorite local bakery. Even Trooper was unsuccessful in enticing her master to join her in a game of fetch. Eve hoped the inspiration from her mother's memory was enough. She hoped this would be the answer to his low mood.

There was no reply from his bedroom, and as far as she could tell, no sounds of movement coming from inside. She considered stomping down the hall and demanding that he get up and join them in the sitting room, but then decided against it. Captain Divine did not respond to bullying. She would talk to the young woman first. Maybe she would learn something in the conversation that she could use to interest him enough to get out of bed.

By the time the young movie star had gotten out of the chauffeured car and up to the front door, Trooper was waiting to welcome her.

"Hello, Trooper!" Megan peeked in and then opened the screen door and greeted the animal that she apparently had previously encountered.

The dog wagged her tail and circled around and around the visitor.

"Yes, I know," Megan said, scratching her under the chin. "I am happy to see you too!"

She stood up and smiled at Evangeline, who had brought out two cups of tea from the kitchen. "Trooper and I became good friends," she noted.

"I see that," Evangeline responded. "Here, come in and have a seat." She watched as the limousine pulled out of the driveway, then turned her attention to her guest, gesturing toward the sofa. She set the cups on the coffee table. "Let me take your coat," she offered.

Megan slid out of her leather jacket and handed it to her host. Evangeline hung it on a hook beside the door.

"I hope you like tea," she said. "I just made a pot. It has a hint of peach in it," she added, taking the seat next to Megan.

"Oh, I love tea," the young woman commented, reaching out and taking a sip from her cup. Trooper had taken her position next to the feet of their guest. "Thanks so much for inviting me." She looked around the room. "Where's Captain Divine?" she asked.

Evangeline smiled. "He's in bed," she answered.

"Oh," was the response. "Is he not feeling well today?"

Evangeline shook her head. "No, he's just stubborn," she answered.

Megan seemed confused.

"He's gotten depressed since he got fitted for his leg," his daughter explained. "I was hoping your visit might cheer him up," she added quietly.

"Well, presently, that would be an unlikely role for me to play," she said.

Evangeline didn't respond.

Megan noticed the confusion. "I'm not sure I am such good company," she acknowledged. "I'm depressed myself."

"What's happened?"

"It's everything," she answered. "First Chaz is missing. Then Chaz is dead. And now . . ." She waved her arm above her head. "Now I'm a suspect in his murder!" She put down the cup of tea and sat back against the sofa. "I can't believe this has happened."

Evangeline sat back as well. "Well, what exactly has been going on?" she asked.

Megan shook her head. "You heard me tell the chief of police that I would come to the police station and tell them what I knew, right?"

Evangeline nodded. She remembered the conversation in the hospital room.

"Well, I went to the station the next day and the interview started fine. I was taken to a room and introduced to a police officer who had a recorder and a pad of paper. He asked for my name and address, just the usual stuff. I thought they needed those things for their files. So I was answering all the questions. One officer even brought me a cup of coffee. It was all perfectly pleasant. And then the detective asked me where I was the day Chaz disappeared. And then he asked if we'd had a fight and if I was angry that Chaz hadn't gotten divorced."

She clasped her hands together and placed them in her lap. "I felt like he was asking me questions that were a little too personal, and I told him I wasn't comfortable talking about those things with a stranger. He said something like he wasn't a stranger, he was a detective investigating a murder. And then I just didn't want to be there anymore, so I asked him if I could leave."

Evangeline waited. "And did he let you?"

"Not at first," she answered. "He kept asking me more questions. And when I wouldn't answer, he said that he would let me go but that he wanted to talk to me again before I returned to California." She shrugged. "But I was planning to go back that night. I was scheduled to audition for a part in a new Mike Nichols movie."

Evangeline didn't respond. She didn't recognize the name.

"It's not the lead," Megan explained. "But Ron, Mr. Polland, got the audition for me. It's a good part. I thought diving back in to work might help take my mind off things."

Evangeline nodded. "So, did you return to Los Angeles?" she asked.

"Yes," she replied. "But a few days later I got a phone call, and the detective ordered me to come back to Santa Fe and answer more questions."

"Ordered?" Evangeline asked. "How did they order you to do that? They haven't made an arrest, have they?"

Megan shook her head. "No. The detective just told me that if I didn't come back to New Mexico and answer their questions here, they would send an L.A. cop out to my house. Well, I didn't want police cars in my driveway or some officer stopping me at a restaurant or out in public or on set. That can ruin a career!"

Evangeline nodded.

"So I came back last week for just a day. And that's when I called Captain Jackson. I thought the first interview was bad, but this was like they really think I'm guilty. I felt as if I was playing a part in some police drama." She shook her head. "They knew practically everything about what I've been doing and who Chaz and I used to see, our old friends." She faced Evangeline. "They'd obviously talked to his ex-wife. There's no telling what she's told them about me."

"Well, what kinds of things did they ask you about that make you think they consider you a suspect?"

"They told me they had some evidence that suggests I know more about how Chaz died than I'm letting on. They said that I was the last one to see him alive."

Evangeline hadn't heard this fact before. "Were you?"

Megan tugged a piece of hair behind her ear. "I guess," she answered. "Well, I mean besides whoever killed him."

"When did you see him last?"

There was a pause before Megan gave a response. "It was the night before he disappeared."

Evangeline studied her guest closely. The answer was not what she expected. She was confused. "Wait, I thought you said you were in California, that you were meeting him at the airport there. I thought you were in Los Angeles while he was here."

"Well, that wasn't exactly the truth," Megan replied. She started picking at her fingernails.

"What is the truth?" Evangeline asked.

"That sounds just like a question that would come from a nun."

The voice coming from the hall startled both women. They glanced up to see Captain Jackson Divine, walking with his crutches, heading in their direction. Evangeline couldn't help but smile. Trooper stirred and gave a bark.

"Way to go, Mom," she muttered under her breath as she got up to give him her place on the sofa.

TWENTY-SEVEN

"You were saying?" the Captain asked. "About you and Chaz?"

"I was here with him," she confessed. "Here in Madrid. We were supposed to get on the plane together and fly to Los Angeles, but he left in his car sometime before the driver was scheduled to come get us. He just never showed back up."

Evangeline leaned the crutches against the wall, walked over to the other side of the room, and sat down in the chair across from the sofa.

"Did you tell the police this information?" he wanted to know.

Megan shook her head. "But they knew it already."

"I guess it wasn't hard to verify that you were on the plane he was supposed to be on going from Santa Fe to Los Angeles instead of waiting at the airport in California for him," he surmised.

"Yeah, I guess," Megan agreed. "Do you think the police talked to the pilot?"

The Captain studied her. "Why? Is there something he might say that would be incriminating?"

She appeared confused. "Incriminating?" she asked.

"Something that raises their suspicions," Evangeline jumped in to explain. "Something that could make you look guilty."

The Captain turned to his daughter, and she lifted her eyebrows in question.

"What?" she asked.

He didn't respond, just gave her a look of annoyance and turned his attention back to their guest. "What kind of information would the pilot have that the police might find interesting?" he asked.

Megan leaned her head back and closed her eyes. She was obviously thinking. She opened her eyes and faced the Captain. She shook her head. "I don't know," she answered unconvincingly.

"Why don't you tell us what happened?" he asked. "And, Megan—" He stopped. "The truth this time."

She rubbed her forehead as if she were getting tired of answering questions. "I woke up and he wasn't anywhere in the house. His car was gone. The driver came to take us to the airport, and I made him wait while I kept calling Chaz's cell phone. I also called the pilot to tell him what had happened and see if he drove himself there. He hadn't. So the driver and I waited for an hour and then went to the airport. I was very upset that Chaz hadn't shown up, and I made the pilot wait a couple more hours, but then I thought that maybe he had just made other arrangements to meet us in L.A. So I had Terrance—the pilot—just go ahead and take off."

It was easy for both Jackson and Evangeline to see that she had more to say.

"Go on, Megan," the Captain pushed.

"I was upset, so just before we left I took a pill to calm down and I fell asleep." She appeared nervous. "He had to wake me up when we got to L.A."

"And what's wrong with that?" Evangeline asked.

The Captain and Megan looked at each other knowingly.

"It doesn't really make her appear that concerned about Cheston if she's taking a nap," Jackson answered and then waited for Megan to add more.

She glanced away. "The pilot, Terrance, he doesn't really like me," she noted. "He's friends with the ex."

The Captain turned to Evangeline. "Cheston's wife," he explained.

She nodded. "Yeah, I figured that one."

"When we landed, Terrance called Mr. Polland, the producer, to tell him that Cheston wasn't on the plane. Mr. Polland told him to turn around and go back and wait for him." She paused. "That's when he woke me up, not until then."

"And what did you do?" the Captain asked.

She shrugged. "I made him wait while I called a few of Chaz's friends to see if they had heard from him, see if he had gotten back to L.A. some other way. And then I called Mr. Polland and asked him to let me go back to try and find him."

"And he said that was okay?" Evangeline asked.

Megan nodded. "He was glad to have me go look for him. Like I've told you, Chaz was costing him a lot of money."

"So the pilot flew you back here?"

She nodded again. "He didn't want to, but after he got on the phone with Mr. Polland, he did."

There was a long pause as everyone seemed to be thinking

about the sequence of events that took place on the day of Cheston's disappearance.

"Why were you afraid to tell me the truth?" the Captain asked.

Evangeline inched forward a bit in her seat. This was a question that bothered her as well.

Megan looked down. "I was the only one with him until the time he left," she responded tearfully. "I flew over from L.A. the day before he was supposed to come home because I thought he was using drugs again, and I thought I could get him cleaned up before he had his meetings. When I got here, I found out he wasn't high. And he was really mad that I came. He said it showed that I didn't trust him and that I was no better than his ex-wife." She reached for the napkin next to her cup of tea. She dabbed at her eyes. "We had a fight and I went to bed." She shook her head. "I don't even know what happened after that except that he got in the hot tub for a while. I never heard him leave and I didn't see him again."

The Captain leaned over and patted her on the arm. "Well, just because you were with him in the house at the time he disappeared, and just because you had a fight with him, and just because you fell asleep on the flight to Los Angeles, that's not enough evidence to arrest you for his murder."

She turned her face aside. Both Evangeline and Jackson noticed the response.

"Megan, that's all they have, isn't it?" he asked.

She didn't answer.

"Megan," he prodded. "What else?"

"Before I left I took some things from the house," she confessed.

Captain Divine locked eyes with her. He waited.

"I was mad at him so I took some of his jewelry."

Evangeline sat back, shaking her head. She didn't know much about solving crimes, but she knew that burglary wouldn't help the young woman's case.

"His ex-wife noticed I was wearing his silver necklace when she saw me at the hospital. It's a little gold-and-silver bear pendant on a silver chain, has some turquoise in it. He bought it on one of his first trips to Santa Fe. She told the police that he never took it off. She told them I stole it."

"And did you?" Evangeline asked.

Megan nodded. "I took it when he was in the hot tub. He always takes it off before he gets in because something in the water tarnishes silver. So after he got in the hot tub, I saw the necklace and took it, along with his bracelet, and went to bed. If he missed them, he didn't come to look for them. I put them in the pocket of my robe. Both the necklace and the bracelet were still there when I woke up. Later, I just put the necklace on and forgot about it."

Captain Divine chimed in. "I remember it," he said. "You had it on when you came by the office."

Megan nodded. "Once I knew something was wrong, I kept wearing it to feel close to him."

"Where is it now?" Evangeline asked.

"The police have it," Megan replied. She reached in her purse that was by her feet. "But I don't think they know about this," she said as she pulled out a wide silver bracelet and placed it on the coffee table.

The doorbell rang, startling all three of them. Evangeline glanced first at the door and then at the table. She was surprised to see that the bracelet had been snatched up by either Megan or the Captain and was already hidden away.

TWENTY-EIGHT

———— ✦✦✦ ————

"I'm looking for Mr. Jackson Divine," the young man said. He was standing on the porch as Trooper and Evangeline waited just inside the screen door.

"It's pronounced *Diveen*," she informed him. "And he's in here." She gestured to her left but didn't yet open the door to invite the visitor in. She was concerned about Megan wanting her privacy, and she wasn't sure of the man's identity or his reason to be standing on the front porch. "Might I tell him who is here to see him?"

The young man seemed confused by the question. "Ma'am?"

"You are?"

"Oh, I'm Ricky. I work with Atlas Prosthetics, and I brought Mr. Divine's, I'm sorry," he said, correcting himself, "Mr. Divine's prosthetic." He hesitated. "We had an appointment for this morning."

Evangeline still didn't open the door. She had forgotten the appointment. And now it wasn't their guest she was worried about. Now she became concerned for the Captain. She wasn't sure this was the best time for the fitting of his new leg. She had just gotten him out of bed, after all, just gotten him interested in something other than what had happened to him. She wasn't sure she wanted to turn his attention back so quickly to his situation, back to his loss.

"For heaven's sake, Eve, let the boy in the house," the Captain shouted.

Evangeline opened the door and Ricky walked in. Trooper gave her greetings and then headed back to sit near the Captain.

The young man glanced over at the sofa, nodding at the two still seated. He didn't seem to recognize Megan.

"So, you got me a new leg?" the Captain asked without getting up.

"Yes, sir," Ricky answered. "It's in the truck. I didn't bring it in because I wanted to make sure it was okay to do the fitting this morning."

"Good a time as any," the Captain replied. "Eve, why don't you take Megan and go get a cup of coffee at Twila's?"

She was being asked to leave. Eve hesitated as Megan jumped to her feet. "Don't you want me to stay and learn with you how to put it on?"

He was shaking his head before she even finished the question. "That's not necessary," he replied. "What did you say your name is, son?" he turned and asked the young man still standing near the door.

"Ricky," he repeated.

"Ricky and I will figure this out together." He winked at the visitor. "Man-to-man," he added.

There was an awkward silence.

"Go on now," the Captain instructed. "I'll be fine. Get yourself one of those chocolate coffees you used to love."

Megan grabbed Evangeline's arm. "Where's the keys to the truck?" she asked. "This'll be my treat."

Evangeline shook her head. She wasn't sure it was the best idea to be away while the prosthetic was being fitted for the first time. She was anxious about what might happen if the Captain became angry or upset. She worried that she might need to stay just to help manage any outburst.

"Evangeline Louise Divine," he said, his voice raised, "I said I'd be fine."

She hesitated. "Okay," she agreed. "We'll be back in an hour. You know where to call if you need me." She retrieved the two coats from the hooks by the door and the keys that were in a bowl on the kitchen counter, as well as a notepad. "We'll be at the Java Junction," she told Ricky as she carefully wrote down a number. "Call me if you need me," she said, handing him the piece of paper.

"A mocha," Megan exclaimed. "That's even better than peach tea!"

Evangeline watched the two men carefully as Megan pulled her out of the house and down the front steps. The two of them got into the truck. Evangeline noticed the young man as he followed behind them and opened the back of the company van. She was driving away as she saw him pulling out a large, narrow box. *The Captain's new leg*, she thought.

"Why are you so worried about him?" Megan asked as they stopped at the end of the driveway before Evangeline pulled out onto the dirt road.

She shook her head. "He's just so hard to get along with," she responded as she carefully made the turn toward town.

"What? No," Megan said. "He's just a big teddy bear."

Evangeline turned to look at her passenger and then turned back to watch the road.

Megan smoothed down the front of her tight jeans. "Does this mean he'll keep my case?" she asked. "And that you'll help him?"

Evangeline hadn't thought of this. "Didn't you get a lawyer?" she asked.

"Sure," Megan replied. "I got one of those as soon as Jack told me to."

Evangeline drove a few miles, signaled, and made the turn into the parking lot of the coffee shop. It was almost lunchtime, well after the morning coffee rush, and there were lots of open spaces.

"Do you think you'll take the case?" Megan asked again.

Evangeline put the truck in park and turned off the engine. She waited a second. There was something else bothering her about the question from the young woman. She realized it wasn't just about the Captain. She was being enlisted to do detective work. Had that been what she'd really had in mind when she asked Megan to visit?

She shook her head. "Megan, I'm not a detective," she replied.

"I know. You're a nun," she responded. "But you and your dad seem to work well together, and I know he'd love to have your help. Besides, the lawyer can only do so much. He can't find out what really happened to Chaz, who really killed him. I need Jackson to work on this. I need you both."

Evangeline opened the door and stepped out of the truck. The young woman followed suit.

"Look, Megan, maybe I made a mistake asking you to come to Madrid." She walked around the truck where the young woman waited. She touched her arm. "I thought your story might get the Captain out of bed, give him something to get interested in, and it seemed to work." She dropped her hand. "But I'm not sure I thought this through well enough. He's not one hundred percent," she explained. "He's got to learn to walk again." She shook her head. "Maybe this isn't the time."

Megan didn't respond right away. She pulled her lipstick out of her purse, blotted her lips with the color. "Maybe you're right," she agreed, placing the tube back in the front pocket of her leather purse. "And I don't want to push your father too hard before he's ready." She glanced around the parking lot. It seemed she wanted to say something else but was unclear how to move forward.

Evangeline noticed the hesitation. "What is it, Megan?" she asked.

"Well, I'm not sure it's really my place to talk about this." She paused, shifted her weight from side to side, fidgeted with her purse. "Sister Evangeline, how much do you know about your father's . . ." She paused again.

Evangeline was interested. She waited.

"Your father's financial situation?"

Evangeline didn't know what she expected to hear, but it wasn't this question. She shrugged and shook her head. "I don't know. Not much, I guess."

"I think I found out something that you might not know, that he doesn't know I know." Megan looked apprehensive. She seemed unsure if she should continue.

"Yes?" Eve asked.

"Eve, I don't know how to tell you this."

Evangeline was getting impatient. She was about to tell the young woman to quit stalling and to spit it out but instead just bit her bottom lip. *Wait*, she told herself. *Be patient.*

"Eve," Megan tried again, "I'm pretty sure the Captain is broke."

TWENTY-NINE

————— ⋅✳⋅✳⋅ —————

"Hey, Sister!" Twila was walking toward the front counter from the rear of the shop. She set the two large cans of coffee she was carrying on the bottom shelf behind her.

"Hello, Twila," Eve responded, reaching her hand across the counter between them. She had not replied to Megan's announcement about the Captain's possible dire financial situation. She had simply turned away from the conversation and walked into the coffee shop.

The woman grabbed the outstretched arm, pulling Evangeline around the counter.

Twila was a large woman and strong. She gave her friend a big hug, finishing it off with a couple of slaps on the back. "You on your bike?" She glanced out the window.

"No, we drove the truck," Eve answered. "Hey, by the way, do you know anything about a yellow cat that's hanging out near the office?"

Twila shook her head. "Nah, that could be anybody's." She winked. "But I'm sure he's yours now."

"It's a she and I really don't need a cat, even though she's quite adorable."

"You haven't needed any of the animals you've had, according to your father, but that never stopped you before."

"Right," Evangeline answered.

"You want to take a ride on my bike later?" Twila asked. She knew how much Evangeline loved to ride.

"I would love to," she replied. "But not just now."

Twila nodded. "How's Captain Jack?" she asked.

"Just fine, Twila, just fine," she replied, trying to catch her breath after having lost it during her friend's greeting. "Thank you for the meat loaf you sent over."

Twila grabbed the dish towel and began wiping away a few crumbs left by the register. "I was going to send a cake but then figured that would be pretty insensitive." She slapped the towel over her shoulder. "With his diabetes and all," she added.

Evangeline smiled. "Meat loaf was a perfect gift. We ate it for two different meals. It was very good."

"Elk meat," the woman noted. "And instead of brown sugar in the sauce, I only used ketchup. It baked up real good."

"I had forgotten the taste of elk," Evangeline commented. "Donnie shoot a buck?"

"Yeah, he got one last year. Had some extra packs in the freezer. I know Captain Jack loves elk meat loaf."

"He did enjoy it."

"The monks and nuns eat much wild game?" Twila asked.

"No, unfortunately we mostly eat a vegetarian diet at the monastery."

"Shame," Twila responded. "How are you managing that? I know how you love a good piece of steak."

Megan cleared her throat and Evangeline turned around, having forgotten she wasn't alone.

"Oh, sorry," she responded and made the introduction: "Twila, this is Megan Flint."

Megan held out her hand.

"I've seen you in here before," Twila noted, taking the outstretched hand and giving it a shake.

"Yes," Megan agreed. "My boyfriend . . ." She hesitated and turned to Evangeline, appearing to need help in finishing her sentence.

Evangeline picked up on the request. "She's from Los Angeles, but she's visited here a few times."

Twila studied the woman closely. She seemed to be trying to figure out exactly when she had seen her before.

Megan smiled and retreated a few steps behind Evangeline.

"We'd like two mochas," Eve placed the order. "Extra cream in mine," she added, glancing over to Megan. "Twila makes the richest whipped cream in the county," she noted.

"You want a little extra, too, Megan?" Twila asked.

"Sure," she answered. "I don't start shooting for a couple of months. I can splurge a little now."

Twila didn't start to make the drinks right away. She was still eyeing Megan. "You're a movie star," she said. "Now I remember. You came in here with your boyfriend a few days before he—" She stopped.

"Before he disappeared," Megan said, finishing the sentence. "Yes, ma'am."

"I heard they found his body over near the Silver Cross," Twila said. She shook her head over and over. "Real shame. I'm sorry, honey," she noted.

There was an awkward pause.

"We haven't had a murder in Madrid in . . ." She stopped to recall. "Gosh, I guess since the gold rush." She grinned. "Lots of killing then," she said and then seemed to notice Evangeline's raised brows, a gesture she took to mean she should quit talking. She pulled out a couple of napkins and handed them to the young women. "So, two mochas, extra cream."

Evangeline headed over to a corner table and Megan followed behind her. The two sat down while Twila became busy making their drinks. Someone else entered the shop, and a new conversation began between the shop owner and the customer.

"Now," Eve began, "what and how do you know about the Captain's finances?"

Megan dropped her purse by her feet, slid her chair closer to Eve, and leaned in with her elbows on the table. "I don't know anything for sure," she said. She sat back. "I overheard a conversation one day. I heard him talking to a banker or somebody about a loan." She placed her hands in her lap. "He didn't know I was there. I had come in the rear entrance because I parked near the fire station and saw that the door was open. And I just overheard him talking about needing the money to pay some bills." She crossed and then uncrossed her legs. "He asked a couple of times, said he had already taken a second mortgage and that this was the only way.

He claimed if he didn't get the loan, he would have to close the business. He sounded pretty upset. I waited a few minutes and then decided I should leave, come in the front door so he could see me. So that's what I did. He never knew I was in there."

Evangeline remembered Dorisanne mentioning something about his debts, about him giving her money to pay off a loan for her husband. She wondered how long this had been going on and, if he was in such serious financial decline, how long he would be able to keep the office open. She also thought about the stack of mail in the cupboard and how it seemed strange that he would keep letters next to coffee cups. They were probably unpaid bills. She shook her head. "Why wouldn't he tell me?"

Megan seemed surprised. "Well, surely you don't have to ask that question, do you? Even I can see that Captain Jackson Divine would never ask for help."

Megan was smarter at reading people than Eve first thought.

"And I don't mean to be too personal, but aren't nuns poor? Is there anything you could actually do to help him?"

Before Evangeline could respond, Twila arrived with their drinks.

"Two mochas with extra cream," she said.

Megan reached for her purse to pay the bill.

Twila waved off the action. "Nope, there's no charge," she explained. "I was going to give you the drinks on the house since you are with my favorite nun, but these are actually compliments of that gentleman right over there." And she turned and gestured to the person who was standing near the front counter.

Both Evangeline and Megan followed her pointed finger to the man. Evangeline was sure that she didn't recognize the short, dark-haired fellow, but when she saw the blush in the other woman's cheeks and her immediate rise from her chair, she knew that Megan certainly did.

THIRTY

"Mr. Polland, this is Sister Evangeline Divine."

Evangeline thought the name sounded familiar.

"He's Chaz's—" Megan stopped. "He was Chaz's producer," she amended.

Evangeline remembered hearing the man's name from past conversations with the young woman.

Twila shrugged as if the news meant nothing to her and returned to the counter.

Evangeline stood up, holding out her hand. "Mr. Polland."

"Please, call me Ron," he said with a smile. He took her hand.

She nodded and sat down.

Megan seemed flustered. "Would . . . would you like to join us?" she asked, stumbling over her words. It was easy to see that the man's presence made her nervous. She glanced down at the table and the two chairs that she and Evangeline had occupied and then looked around as if she were scanning the room for a bigger table or one with more chairs.

Polland appeared to understand what she was considering and reached behind him to pull the chair over that was closest to him. "Please, Megan, take your seat, drink your coffee."

She smiled nervously, sat in her chair, and lifted the cup to her lips.

Evangeline thought the young woman drank as if the man's words had been an instruction and not merely a means of kindness. She watched Megan and then lifted her eyes to the man who had paid for her mocha. Before she had the chance to thank him for the drink, Twila brought him a cup of coffee and stood behind him, grinning. Evangeline thought she might pull up another chair.

"It's a two-shot espresso with soy milk," she announced to the threesome at the table. She remained where she was.

Evangeline smiled and nodded. She took a sip of her mocha. "Well, mine's perfect," she noted.

Polland was watching Megan. He hadn't touched the cup Twila had just placed in front of him and didn't seem to notice that the proprietor stood waiting for him to take a sip and give his approval.

There was a pause.

"Will there be anything else?" Twila finally asked, realizing her customer wasn't going to try his drink. The three of them shook their heads, and she rolled her eyes and headed back to the counter.

"So, Megan dear," the man said with a smooth, fatherly tone, "when did you leave Los Angeles?"

She didn't meet his eyes, but when she lifted her face, a small dab of cream was on the end of her nose.

Evangeline noticed it right away and didn't know whether to hand her a napkin or gently tell her to wipe her face. Before she could make a decision, however, Mr. Polland had made his own, pulling out the handkerchief from his front right breast pocket and removing the dollop of cream from her face himself. The young woman jerked back quickly as if his movement somehow frightened her. Evangeline stared at the two of them.

"I'm sorry, dear. You stuck your nose in the cream and made a little mess."

Megan remained quiet.

He turned to face Evangeline. "So, did I hear Megan right?" he asked. "Did she introduce you as Sister?" He smiled.

"Yes, I'm a nun in the religious order known as the Benedictines."

"After Saint Benedict of Nursia," he replied.

Evangeline was surprised. "Are you Catholic, Mr. Polland?"

"Ron," he reminded her. "Lapsed." He winked. "I actually went to seminary for three years. Trained by the Jesuits," he noted and finally took a sip of his espresso. "Turns out I'm not quite disciplined enough for the lifestyle."

She nodded.

"You were going to be a priest?" Megan spoke up, sounding surprised.

He smiled. "Priest, producer . . . They're actually not that different."

Evangeline was curious. "How is that?" she wanted to know.

"Well, the way I see it, running a movie studio is like running a church."

She waited for more of an explanation.

He complied. "The worship service, it's not much different than a film."

"I never quite thought of things that way," Evangeline said.

"Well, they're pretty similar if you think about it. There's an agreeable script, faith that it will come together, music to accent the drama, lights, sound, props. There are roles to fill, lines to learn, and at the end of the day, you hope there's enough money so that the bills get paid and there's a little left over." He paused. "Oh, and with all your work and dedication, you hope that the audience gets a nice show."

Evangeline didn't know how to respond. She hadn't ever heard the work of a priest or the life of a community of faith stripped down to such an uninspired existence. She took another sip of her drink and looked away.

"So, Meg." The man seemed ready to move on to another subject.

The young woman snapped to attention.

"What has brought you back to this little godforsaken town?"

She looked at Evangeline and then back at him. "I, uh, I . . ."

"She knew my father," Eve answered for her. "He's just gotten home from the hospital, and she came to see how he is doing."

The man studied Megan and then smiled. He sat back, appearing to relax. "Megan is a conscientious girl," he noted.

"He was the one helping me find Chaz," Megan piped up. "Evangeline's father," she added.

Polland nodded knowingly. "And now Chaz has been found."

Megan turned away. Polland moved closer to Megan. "Meg, seeing as how we're both here at the same time, why don't we head back to Santa Fe together? We'll fly to L.A. on the jet and we can have a nice, long chat this afternoon."

She fumbled with her response. "But I have a car, a driver. And I flew commercial."

"Nothing to worry about. I saw Matthew in the parking lot earlier. He stopped for coffee. I've already dismissed your driver so you'll be able to ride with me. And you can cancel the flight." He smiled and patted Megan on the hand. "Save those frequent-flier points for another trip."

Polland drank all his espresso in one gulp and put down his cup. He stood and threw a twenty-dollar bill on the table before turning to face Evangeline. He held out his hand.

Evangeline remained seated but took the man's hand.

"Pleasure, Sister."

She smiled. "Nice meeting you, too, Mr. Polland." She looked over at Megan, but the young woman would not meet her eyes.

THIRTY-ONE

——◈◈◈——

Evangeline called and checked on the Captain. He was still working with Ricky and then planned to go out to lunch in Santa Fe with Daniel, so she knew she had some time on her own. She finished her mocha and then took Twila up on her offer. The bike was a 1984 Harley Low Glide, candy-red, the same one that Twila had bought new when Eve was just a teenager. It was the first motorcycle Eve had ever been on, and she was glad to find out her friend still had it and that she had the chance to take it out for a short ride.

Along with the keys, Twila had also handed Eve her leather jacket and helmet, but the nun had declined the helmet. She took the jacket, however, knowing that the coat she was wearing wouldn't keep her warm. Besides, she wanted to enjoy the feel of wearing leather again. She had given away all but one of her riding jackets when she joined the monastery, but she'd kept a couple of good pairs of boots, which were perfect for riding and which she just happened to be wearing when Megan showed up.

She looked around the parking lot and decided to head north. She adjusted the mirrors, turned on the engine, and kicked it into high gear, speeding up the highway. Immediately, she began to unwind.

As she drove along the familiar road, Eve wondered why Ron Polland appeared to have such a hold over Megan. Her response to his presence seemed to be more than just simple respect for the man who obviously had some say about her career in film—the young woman seemed to be afraid of him. She hadn't even tried to get out of going back to Los Angeles with him, nor had she mentioned saying good-bye to the Captain for her when she left. Polland made the suggestion that she join him, she made one very lame attempt to refuse, and then she had jumped at the command. *What else did the Hollywood producer ask from the young star?* Evangeline wondered. *What other commands had he given her?*

She sped along the Cerrillos Hills, enjoying the wind in her hair, the sun on her face, and thought more of the way Polland treated Megan, the way he seemed to be able to control her. Eve knew herself well enough to know that submission was not a strong suit for her. She had been cautioned on more than one occasion as a child about her issues with authority. That had been a source of much trouble in her home and at school. And then, even as a young woman at the monastery, she had received counsel regarding her strong will. She had been told by her superiors repeatedly that she was difficult to supervise because she demonstrated a clear resistance to authority, however benevolent.

She slowed down, making the turn toward Galisteo, and recalled one of the more recent conversations she'd had with the vice superior, in which she had questioned the new order making the nuns leave the main campus.

"Don't you realize that obedience to your superiors is a manifestation of your willingness to obey God?"

"I do," she had answered.

"And don't you see that learning to obey the order of the monastery as well as our supervision teaches you the humility you need to obey the commands of God?"

"I do," she repeated.

"Then why do you struggle so fiercely with the instructions you are given by your superiors?"

"I don't think my struggles are fierce."

Brother Oliver had not responded right away.

"Sister Eve," he had finally said with a great deal of gentleness. "We submit to the church and to God because it is in submission that we are taught humility, and humility leads us to the cardinal virtue of temperance. If one is unable to submit to God and to the legitimate authority of the church, then one can never truly attain temperance. And as members of the religious order, we are called to work toward this virtue because in attaining it we are led to the restraint or expression of the inordinate movements of our desires or appetites."

He had studied her at this point, and she had become uncomfortable with the attention.

"I will do better," she had responded.

He waited. "Sister Eve, it is not so much that we are requesting that you do better as it is that you understand your resistance."

She sighed. She wanted desperately to be finished with this conversation and to be dismissed.

"We submit to authority because we love God, because we

desire to serve God, not because we just want to do better and stay out of trouble. We submit as a response to our call to follow Christ."

"I don't understand," she confessed because clearly she didn't. "Do you want me to submit and not argue as much or not? Do you just want me to accept this new edict and not state my opinion?"

He had smiled at that. "I want you to have the desire to submit, not to placate your superiors, not to get us off your back, but rather I want you to make the choice to submit because it is your deepest desire to obey and to serve. And I want you to accept what is inevitable."

Evangeline took a right down a dirt road. She knew a shortcut back to town. After some time she had finally come to understand what the vice superior had been trying to teach her, and from then on, she had worked hard on her response to instructions from those in charge. But she could never become as submissive as the others in the community. She also knew that she would never be like Megan. No man would ever cause her to cower the way Ron Polland had made the young star cower. One day, she might ultimately learn the way of submission and obedience as a means to humility, but cowering was simply not an option for Sister Evangeline Divine.

She pulled in to the parking lot at Twila's and turned off the engine. When she stood up from the bike and dropped the kickstand, she heard a familiar voice.

"Well, if it isn't the Harley-riding nun herself."

THIRTY-TWO

—— ❖ ——

"Mother Madeline!"

The two women ran toward each other and into a big embrace.

"What a lovely surprise!" Evangeline stood back, smiling at her mentor and friend Reverend Madeline Barr, an Episcopal priest who served a small parish in Los Alamos, outside Santa Fe. "What are you doing in Madrid?"

The older woman smiled. "Your father didn't tell you?" She had a cup of coffee in her hand.

"Tell me what?"

"I retired and moved back at the end of the year. I bought Ned Shelley's homeplace out near Cedar Hill."

Eve knew the area well. Ned Shelley, a longtime resident of Madrid, had passed away a couple of years earlier. He left the property his family had homesteaded since the early 1930s to a distant family member in another state, who immediately put it on the market. "But why didn't I hear about a retirement party or some event at the church?"

Madeline shrugged. "Aw, I didn't want any of that hoopla. All those speeches about enjoying the golden years, those little, dainty white-bread sandwiches, and people who've given you heartburn for twenty years suddenly showing up and pretending they're your best friends. Nah, I didn't want any of that." She waved her hands in front of her. "I just asked the vestry to help me make the down payment on the house and told them we'd have a party out there this summer." She smiled. "And what about you, Sister Eve? What are you doing back in town?"

"The Captain," she replied. "He had to have part of his leg amputated a few weeks ago. According to Dorisanne, it's my turn to take the parental caregiving shift."

"I didn't know," she replied. "I'm sorry to hear that. I hope he's doing well."

Eve shrugged. "He's about as well as you'd expect him to be."

Madeline nodded. "I see you're still riding."

"It's Twila's," Evangeline said. "Let me give these keys back to her and if you want, we'll drive over to the Captain's place. I wanted to pick up the mail and check the office."

"I'll wait out here for you," the older woman replied.

Eve went inside, gave the keys and jacket back to Twila with her thanks for the ride, and returned to her friend. The two of them got in the truck and headed down the road to the detective agency office. They got out and Eve found the key and opened the door. The cat from the street hurried up to them.

"You're still keeping strays, I see." Madeline stood at the door.

"They just keep following me," she replied. "This is Daisy," she added.

"Some things never change," Madeline noted, watching the cat as it made its way inside.

"Please, please, come in." Eve moved aside so that Madeline could enter. "Let me clean off a couple of seats and we can sit down." She removed the magazines and mail from the two folding chairs in front of the Captain's desk and dusted them off. She turned them around so that they were facing each other and then patted one. The old two-room office was far from fancy, but Eve had come to love the place. She had cleaned it and rearranged the few pieces of furniture, giving it a more spacious feel. The room now had a familiarity and warmth to it that welcomed folks to sit down and tell their stories.

Madeline glanced around the office after they had taken their seats. "So this is what a private detective agency looks like."

Evangeline smiled. "It's what this private detective agency looks like anyway." Madeline crossed her legs at the ankles and took a sip from her coffee. "And how are you?" she asked.

"I'm fine," Eve answered. The cat jumped up in her lap, and she gave the animal a good scratch behind the ears.

"They gave you a leave of absence from the monastery?" Madeline asked.

Eve nodded. "Two months."

Madeline raised her eyebrows. "That's a good, long time," she said.

"It was a surprise, actually," Eve responded.

The older woman waited. She was never one to force a comment or conversation.

"When Mama was sick, you know, they wouldn't let me leave." Eve recalled telling Mother Madeline all this before. The

Episcopalian had been Eve's spiritual director when she was in the discernment process of becoming a nun.

Madeline offered an empathetic nod.

Eve shrugged. "But for some reason, the vice superior agreed this time."

"Could be that it actually is in God's hands, as the saints all say."

"Could be they were glad to get rid of me. You know about the changes, right?"

"I heard they were making the monks and nuns separate." She shook her head. "How long have the men and women been living together there?"

"Since the seventies," Eve answered.

"This came down from the Vatican?" Madeline wanted to know. Eve nodded.

"Then I guess there's no fighting it."

"Guess not," Eve answered softly.

"And how is your father? Is he in a rehabilitation facility? Did the surgery go as planned?"

"The surgery went well, but the Captain informed his doctor and care team that he would not be using their recommended facility. He's home," she answered. She let the cat down and watched as she walked over to the little bed Eve had made for it in the corner of the room.

Madeline lifted her chin and gave a laugh. "Then it seems as if the vice superior and the Vatican had a bit of divine guidance in letting you leave the community. You are needed in Madrid."

"It certainly seems that way."

"So, are you doing some work for the agency?" Madeline asked, looking over at the Captain's desk.

Eve turned and noticed the clutter of papers and mail. She shook her head. "I hadn't planned on it, but he could use a little assistance in here."

"Does he have a case?"

"Well, that's not exactly clear," Eve answered. "Did you hear about the murder?"

Madeline stiffened. "In Madrid?"

"Cerrillos, actually. But the man had been staying here in Madrid. He rented that house that used to be a bed-and-breakfast in the nineties, the one way out there near the rock garden that the couple from New York started."

"Rising Son?" Madeline asked.

Eve nodded.

"I thought they closed."

"They did as a bed-and-breakfast business, but apparently Hollywood types have been renting it." Eve paused. "Evidently they shoot a lot of movies out here."

"I did know that," Madeline said. "And I also heard some of the Hollywood and artistic types were renting and buying up the property around here. I thought I'd get a deal on Shelley's place, but it turns out that because of the Californians moving here, I had to pay the asking price."

"Was someone else looking to buy it?"

"The guy who bought the property below it. He's a writer. And I think he may write movie scripts."

"Oh yeah?" Eve was interested. "And who is that?"

"Biltmore is his last name," Madeline replied. "I only met him once. I stopped by to introduce myself when I moved in. He was typing away when I knocked on the door, and he said he was working on a project. He seemed to be in a big hurry so I didn't stay." She thought for a moment. "Ross Biltmore," she said. "That was it. And there was another guy there too," she added. "I never saw him, just saw a fancy silver BMW in the driveway and thought I hadn't noticed that car before when I'd passed by the place. I heard Mr. Biltmore call out his name. Let's see, seems like the name was, Chance or Chap, something strange like—"

"Chaz?" Evangeline asked.

Madeline smiled. "That's it," she said. "Mr. Biltmore's friend was named Chaz."

THIRTY-THREE

Evangeline was home when the Captain returned from his lunch with Daniel. She heard the car and hurried to the kitchen window. She watched as he got out of the passenger's seat, leaned against his crutches, said his good-byes, and hobbled to the door.

The disappointment hit quickly. He was not wearing the prosthetic. She hurried to the door when she heard the horn blow.

Daniel leaned out the window. "He's as strong as an ox," he shouted. "And stubborn as a mule," he added, tooting the horn and backing out.

Eve waved and when she turned around, her father was shaking his fist at his former partner. "Welcome home," she said.

He grunted as he walked past.

"So, how was lunch?" she asked, closing and latching the screen door.

"Horseman's Haven," he answered. "Green chile burger and cheese fries." He moved inside the house, balancing himself against the wall as Trooper ran into the room to greet him. He gave the dog a loving pat, placed his crutches against the wall, and hopped over to the sofa.

Eve just watched. *Where is the prosthetic?* she wondered, but she didn't ask. "That sounds healthy."

He waved away the comment. He was breathing heavier than usual, and Eve could see the trip had tired him.

"You want a glass of water?"

He nodded and she went into the kitchen to fetch the drink.

"Did you see any of your old buddies?" She handed him a glass.

"Sam Rogers, Cecil Rodriquez, Louie . . ." He paused, breathing. "The usuals," he added, rubbing his forehead.

"You want to take a nap?"

He shook his head. "I think I'd just like to sit here." He took a big swig of his drink.

Eve took a seat across from him. "See anybody else from work?"

"Nobody special," he answered. "You look like the cat that ate the canary. What are you so happy about?"

"I met an interesting person this morning."

He waited.

"Ron Polland," she announced.

The name didn't seem to register at first.

"Chaz Cheston's producer," she added.

"He was in Madrid?"

"At Twila's," she confirmed. "He came in while Megan and I were having our coffee." She shook her head. "There's something strange between the two of them."

"Strange like what?" He finished off his water.

"Strange like, I don't know," she said.

"Give me a little more than that, would you?" he responded. He looked around the room. "Did Megan introduce you?"

"Yes. Then she left," Eve answered. "With him. It was weird. He came in after we did, but it was almost like he was looking for her, like he deliberately came to Madrid to find her. He had even sent her driver back to Santa Fe without asking her."

"Maybe he was paying for the driver."

Eve shook her head. "No, I don't think that was it. She flew here commercial, so I figure she was paying for the car service too."

"Then maybe he's just protective of her, heard she had come back and he came to town to make sure she was okay, get her back to Los Angeles. Maybe he doesn't want her to be around here because he knows the police are interested in her."

"And are they?"

He nodded. "They've narrowed down their list of suspects dramatically. The chief made Wallace Hinds lead detective, and the guys say he's convinced the mistress is the murderer."

"What's supposed to be her motive?"

"She was his mistress," he answered.

"That doesn't seem like a good motive for murder," Eve said.

"It is if he's still married and had lied about getting a divorce. Apparently, there are some witnesses that say she was pretty angry at him before she came back here. One witness will even testify that she went to the Los Angeles County Courthouse to look through the public divorce records. Evidently she stole from him and she was the last one to see him alive. Not to mention that she lied to the police the first time they questioned her." He shook his head.

"Well, that all sounds pretty circumstantial," Eve commented.

"There's more. She also had access to the drug found during the autopsy. Her brother's a veterinarian, works in San Diego. Vets have that drug readily available, and she made a visit to see him a month or so ago. She has all the DVDs of that television show she told you about, the one where the guy paralyzes his victims with the M99. She's definitely in trouble. I just hope she's got a good attorney."

"She's got you," Eve said, eyeing him for his response.

"That's what everybody seems to think."

She waited for the explanation.

"Megan told Hinds that I was working for her."

"Why would she do that?"

"Guess she thought it might make them ease up on her." He grinned. "She didn't realize that Hinds doesn't really care for me. So her strategy actually backfired."

"What did you do to Hinds?" she asked.

He met her eyes. "Why do you ask it like that?"

"You know what I mean," she replied. "Why doesn't he like you?"

"I may have made him mad before I left."

Eve shook her head but chose not to ask for details. "So, did you decide to help her?"

"Yeah, I did. You know I like the kid, and I don't think she's guilty of murder, and then when I heard this gives me the chance to piss off both the chief and Wallace, how could I refuse?"

Eve wasn't sure if this was good news or bad. She glanced down at his missing foot, deciding to ask the question she had been wanting to ask since he got home. "The prosthetic didn't work?"

He looked down as well, shook his head. "It's no good."

She slid down in her chair, defeated. If he had made up his mind not to use the prosthetic, then there was nothing she could do to change it. She would have to figure out how to help him adjust to life using crutches. "Did it just not fit or did it hurt? Was there something wrong with Ricky?"

"Nah, nothing like that," he answered. "I like Ricky, invited him for supper next Friday."

"Then what's the problem?"

"I didn't like the skin color."

Eve was confused.

"They had some pasty white foot attached to a brace. I told him to take it back and get me a brown foot. I got Spanish blood. I can't have a pasty white foot. The new one will be here next week."

THIRTY-FOUR

Megan's arrest made all the headlines. It was the topic of conversation on the entertainment television news shows and even made most editions of the national network nightly news programs. She was charged with murder, arraigned, and released on an extremely high bail, but was ordered to stay in New Mexico, a sort of house arrest.

Ron Polland flew back with her and her attorney to Santa Fe at the time she was arrested, arranged bail, and even found a house, which Eve suspected *he* rented, for her to stay in while she awaited the trial. He had suddenly become the most loyal supporter of the Hollywood actress and seemed never to leave her side.

Once the contract had been written up and signed both by Megan's attorney, a Mr. Lee McDonald, well-known lawyer to the stars, and the Captain, the Divine Private Detective Agency was back in business. Evangeline instantly became driver, secretary, bookkeeper, and assistant. She had promised to get the office on

Firehouse Lane in order, continue to tidy the place up a bit, and shuttle her father back and forth to Santa Fe since he had not yet been cleared to drive, but she had not realized she had also agreed to work alongside him. The details of the business arrangement between lawyer and private detective were clear and spelled out in a binding contract. The details of a nun assisting her ailing but recuperating father had never been discussed.

"The first thing we need to find out is where Cheston was going when he left his house the morning he was scheduled to be in Los Angeles." The Captain was sitting on the edge of his bed while Ricky knelt in front of him strapping on the new prosthetic.

This was the third attempt. The second one, though pigmented to the Captain's specifications, turned out to be a woman's ankle and foot. Once the Captain saw it, he wouldn't allow the young man from Atlas Prosthetics in the house, even though Evangeline teased him that having a woman's lower leg might improve his chances of "getting his foot back in the door" at the Santa Fe police station.

Once the chief of police and Wallace Hinds found out that Divine was working for the accused murderer, everyone on the force was barred from having any communication with the former police detective. Even Daniel limited his contact with Jackson to outside of work and on his own time. He told his ex-partner that he was being watched closely by his superiors and couldn't risk talking to him on company time.

"If we can find out where he was going that morning before flying back to L.A. and whom he might have seen, then we will have a huge piece of this mystery solved. We'd probably even have the killer."

Eve was sitting in the chair across from the two men, taking notes. "Maybe he left the night before," she said. "Remember Megan said she never saw him after he was in the hot tub. Maybe he got out, saw that she was asleep in his bed, and left the house then."

"No, that's not what happened."

Eve was confused. "But if she was the only one at the house, then she's the one who saw him last, and she said that she didn't see him again after he was in the hot tub."

"Turns out she recanted that part of the story too," he responded.

"What? When?" Eve asked, shaking her head.

Megan's story had already gone through several revisions since they first met. Evangeline liked Megan a lot, fully believed in her innocence, and was committed to clearing her name, but she was beginning to worry about the young woman's understanding of what it meant to tell the truth.

"When I talked to her last week after she was arrested, she said she got up at around three in the morning and that Cheston was asleep in the guest room."

Evangeline blew out a long breath. "Is there anything else in her story that she's changed?"

"Oww!" the Captain yelled. "Ricky, that's tender under there!"

Trooper, who had been resting at the foot of the bed, rose up.

"Sorry. I'll take it down a notch so it's not so tight." Ricky adjusted one of the straps on the prosthetic. "There." He sat back on his haunches. "How's that, Mr. Divine?"

The Captain nodded. "Better," he answered, still seated. "I got a copy of her police report. Her statement is in the file. We went over it and she said that what is written on this statement is the truth. They had dinner and then an argument. She went into the bedroom and stayed a couple of hours, and then she saw him in the hot tub about eleven o'clock. She went to bed and got up at three. She went to find him and he was asleep in the guest room."

Evangeline opened up the file in her lap and began rifling through the papers, searching for Megan's statement. "By the way, it's *Diveen*," she said to Ricky. "Not Divine, *Diveen*."

"Right," he replied. He had certainly heard the correct pronunciation before.

Eve continued. "So, what time did Megan say she got up to get ready for the flight? What time did she notice he was gone?"

"O six hundred," came the answer.

"So, Cheston left the house sometime between three and six." Evangeline was putting the facts together. She thought for a minute. "Did he have his car here in Madrid?"

The Captain nodded. "According to everyone who remembers, he drove from Los Angeles a month or so before disappearing. He bought a new BMW after the last rehab stint."

Mother Madeline had mentioned seeing the same brand of car in the driveway of her neighbor, the writer. "Was it silver?"

The Captain turned to his daughter. "How did you know?"

"Madeline saw a silver BMW a couple of months ago. It was parked at the house below her property." She shrugged. "Do you think it could be the same one?"

"Well, you grew up in Madrid. How many fancy, new European cars do you see in town?" He sat up a bit, sliding a little closer to the edge. "Find out what Madeline knows about her neighbor. Maybe it's somebody the police missed."

Ricky moved back, giving the Captain more room to try standing. Trooper paid close attention to her master's movements.

Evangeline looked up from the file and joined the other two witnesses to watch the patient stand for the first time on his new leg.

He positioned his hands behind him on the bed and pushed. He stood for a second. He grimaced a bit and then exhaled. "Well, Ricky, let's take Peggy for a trial run."

"Peggy?" Evangeline shook her head.

"I know this is a man's ankle and foot, and I realize that Ricky has brought me one that is a lot fancier than a wooden leg, but Peggy works and Peggy she is." He stepped out with his good leg and then slowly and carefully put weight on the prosthetic. He nodded and took another step. "Trooper, you and I can finally start taking those hikes again!" And he headed out of his bedroom and into the hall, the dog loping behind.

Evangeline looked over to Ricky, who was grinning.

"Peg leg, Peggy . . . that's a good one," he noted. "Your dad's pretty funny."

"Hilarious," she replied, and they both followed the Captain out the door.

THIRTY-FIVE

————— ⟨✦⟩ —————

"It's his car all right. Hold on a minute."

There was a pause.

"Sorry. I needed to walk around the corner from the station. Lots of nosy cops around here. Anyway, they found the BMW out near Cedar Hill, out along one of the old mining roads. No prints anywhere except the victim's. No cell phone or laptop. Whoever drove it out there must have gotten a ride out or hiked back to town. But with the snow and the extended time since the murder, there aren't any tracks of note."

The Captain nodded and jotted down a few notes while listening on the telephone to his friend's news. He was sitting at his desk.

Evangeline sat across from him, paying close attention.

"What have you heard about that known acquaintance of the victim named Ross Biltmore?" he asked. "The writer?"

Evangeline leaned forward, trying to hear the response. Madeline hadn't seen any activity near the place since she'd returned from her cruise. She didn't think he was in town. Evangeline drove to the edge of Biltmore's property but was unable to get through the locked gate. She talked to the realtor who had sold the property, too, but the only thing he would say was that Mr. Biltmore saw the place and made an offer the next day. He had accepted the terms of the sale and didn't ask for any changes to the purchasing contract. "It was the easiest fifteen thousand I've ever made," he'd said.

The Captain dropped the receiver from his mouth, covering it with his hand. "Can you get me a cup of coffee?" he asked. "And can you get that cat out of here?"

Evangeline rolled her eyes. She was not about to push the cat out, and besides, she thought he was going to bring her up to speed as to what was going on by repeating what Daniel was saying about Madeline's neighbor. She stood up and walked over to fix him a cup of coffee.

"You say he left to go out of town a day before Cheston disappeared?" He winked at Evangeline as she handed him the cup.

She sat back down.

"Yes, fax it over," he said. "Thank you, Dan," he added before hanging up the phone.

Evangeline waited for the rest of the news from the police.

The Captain took a sip of his coffee. He was taking his time.

"A helicopter pilot spotted the car. It was way out past your friend's place, way down one of the old mining roads." He nodded. "But it's definitely his."

"And Mr. Biltmore?" she asked.

He shook his head. "Out of the country is all they know.

Airplane ticket for New Delhi the day before Cheston disappeared. No return date confirmed."

"What do they know about him?"

He shrugged. "A writer, but no published book."

"Screenplays?"

"Not purchased."

"Well, he had money coming in from somewhere," Eve said.

The Captain studied her. "How's that?"

"He paid cash for the house and land," she replied, recalling what the realtor had told her. "And the property sold for half a million dollars."

"That old cabin?" he asked, sounding surprised.

"The cabin and fifty acres," she explained. "It belonged to the Placer Mining Company. Biltmore owns the land all the way from Madeline's property line to the highway."

"When did he buy it?"

"Couple of years ago," she answered. "Right after that movie came out that put Madrid on the map."

"The motorcycle one," he said.

"Twila said she met John Travolta."

The Captain reached inside his drawer and pulled out an autographed picture of the movie star. It was signed, "Thanks for solving the mystery."

Evangeline read it and looked up. "What mystery did you solve?"

"They were shooting out past the Silver Cross, and I drove him to where they were filming one day. He couldn't figure out how to open the ranch gate."

"The sliding bar?"

The Captain nodded. "Guess they don't have those in Hollywood." He opened the drawer and placed the picture back in it. "Anyway, I had to get out and show him how to open it."

Evangeline nodded and then thought about something. "Those gates are on just about all the properties around here."

"Yep, some cowboy design, I reckon."

"And not everyone knows how to open them. I remember you teaching me and Dorisanne how to reach around and slide it without pinching our fingers."

The Captain looked at her. "Right."

"I just thought of something," she said.

He waited.

"The gate at Mr. Biltmore's property."

"It has that kind of lock?"

"It does. And it wasn't secured the right way." She began to remember how there was a chain lock on the gate, but the slide was unfastened. The chain merely wrapped around the last bar of the gate and around the first bar of the fence.

"So, somebody locked it and didn't know what they were doing?" The Captain picked up on what she was suggesting.

There was a pause.

"Could have been the police," she suggested.

He shook his head. "Daniel said the same thing you did. They drove out there but couldn't get in. They didn't have a warrant, so they didn't bust the lock."

"So, somebody left the property, wrapped the chain lock back, but didn't close the gate correctly."

"I guess it could have been Biltmore," the Captain said.

Evangeline shook her head. "He's lived there more than a year. Surely he figured out how to close and lock the gate at some point in all that time."

"You're suggesting somebody went out there and messed with the gate while Biltmore has been gone?"

She shrugged. "Could be. And there's something else that bothers me."

"I'm listening," he responded.

"If they still think Megan did this, how do they suppose she killed him, disposed of his body, abandoned his car, and got back to the house? They seem to be overlooking something very important."

"Megan doesn't drive." The Captain grinned and pointed his finger at Evangeline. "You are turning out to be a fine detective!"

Even though she had spent a lot of years trying to overcome the original and most deadly of the seven sins, Evangeline couldn't help herself. The Captain's words flooded her with a sense of pride. She smiled and then, quickly recognizing her temptation, bowed her head to pray.

THIRTY-SIX

John Ewing was standing in his kitchen. Evangeline could see him as they walked toward the house.

"No, I'm calling from the home phone. I know. I know . . . I won't talk long."

There was a moment of silence.

"His girlfriend," he said. "The young Hollywood star that used to come to New Mexico with him."

Evangeline and Captain Divine had parked at the stables. When they didn't find anyone around there, they headed up to the house. They were standing at the front door and could overhear the phone conversation. Evangeline glanced at the Captain and gave a shrug, suggesting they might be interrupting something important. "Maybe we should go back to the stables," she whispered.

"Hold on just a minute."

And suddenly Ewing was at the door. "I'm going to have to call you back," he said and quickly turned off the cordless phone. "Hello, Jack," he said, pushing open the screen door. "What a nice surprise."

Jackson and Evangeline moved aside so that the rancher would have room to walk out. When he did, he spotted the woman.

"Sister," he said. "Well, what a treat."

She smiled. "Mr. Ewing, good to see you too." She reached out and gave the man a hug.

He clapped her on the back and then stepped back. "So, how long have you both been standing out here?"

He seemed a little nervous.

"We just walked up," the Captain answered. "We parked down there," he added and turned and pointed to his truck. "Thought you might be in your office." His voice was calm, easy. He sounded like someone who was just stopping by to see a friend.

The rancher glanced out toward his friend's truck and then back. "Nice day today," Captain Divine said.

"Ah, yes, it looks like spring is on its way." He nodded.

"Good day for a ride," Jackson noted.

Ewing studied him. "You want to go horseback riding?"

"Oh no." Jackson laughed. "I reckon my riding days are over." He stuck out his prosthetic.

Ewing looked down at the artificial limb. He suddenly seemed embarrassed. "I was sorry to hear about your operation," he said.

"Oh, it was nothing. I'm doing very well," Jackson replied, waving off the sympathy. "Good hospital over there at Santa Fe. And now that I got this contraption, I'll be just fine."

Ewing nodded and turned his attention to Evangeline. "How are things at the convent, Sister?" he asked. "You sure aren't dressed like the last time I saw you at church."

"Things are fine," she answered, looking down at the clothes she was wearing, the old shirt from her father's closet, a pair of faded jeans, the boots. She hadn't worn her habit since the day she left Pecos.

There was an awkward pause as all three of them nodded and smiled at one another.

"If I remember right, you used to know how to handle a horse pretty well when you and your sister were young."

Eve grinned. "Yes, sir, we had our own horses when we were little."

"Eve was a barrel racer until she discovered motorbikes."

Ewing nodded. "That's right. I remember seeing you once or twice over at the county rodeo. You won a few ribbons."

"That was a long time ago," she noted.

An extended thread of silence elapsed before the rancher made another comment.

"Well, you know, Captain, I've read about folks doing about anything they want without arms and legs. Skiing, hiking, swimming. So, if you want to try getting on a horse, I'm happy to help you."

"No, no. We're not here to ride," he said.

The rancher waited. "I'm sorry. Where are my manners?" he asked and opened the screen door. "Would you like to come in, have a glass of tea or a beer or something?"

"Thanks, but we didn't come to mess up your day." Jackson waved his hands in protest.

Ewing closed the door and stood with them on the porch.

"We were just wondering if you could tell us where they found the body."

Eve was surprised. On the ride over to the Silver Cross, the

Captain had made it sound as if he was going to ask the question in passing, just take the stance of a curious bystander. They had both agreed not to tell folks around town that Jackson was working for Megan. He had explained that sometimes people talk more when they think they're not being interviewed.

Ewing looked first at the Captain, then at Evangeline.

"Why would you want to know about that?" he asked.

"Oh, you know, Eve and I were just arguing about where he was. One of my old buddies on the force told me he was found out near the cemetery, and Eve shared that somebody in town said he was out next to the road, by the wash. You know me . . ." He grinned. "I hate to be wrong, so since we were just heading home from Santa Fe, I told her to stop in here so that I could prove I was right."

Ewing studied his guests. "Well, looks like this may be a first," he finally said.

"And why's that?" Jackson asked.

"Your daughter's got the correct information this time. You're wrong."

"Oh?" Eve smiled.

"The body was found off the side of the road heading up to the mines trail. Aaron saw it when he was on top of the hill. Snow had melted so he got a good look." He paused. "You want to ride up there to see it?" he asked. "I can get the four-wheeler."

Jackson shook his head. "Nah, that's all right. I know where you're talking about. I guess being wrong was bound to happen sooner or later." He nodded, sticking his hands in the pockets of his jacket.

"Always lots of rumors getting started in a situation like this."

"Did you know the guy?" Jackson asked.

Ewing seemed a bit surprised by the question. "The dead man?"

"Yeah, he was a Hollywood director, Charles Cheston. He ever come out here to ride?"

Evangeline watched the rancher closely. She wanted to see how he responded.

"I heard he rented a place for a couple of months, seemed to like it out here, and I was just wondering if he ever came over to try a little horseback riding," Jackson pressed.

Ewing shook his head. "No, he never came out for a ride." He folded his arms across his chest. "Get a lot of those Hollywood types, though."

"Yeah, I figured," Jackson responded. "Come out here and want a taste of the cowboy life."

"You won't hear no complaint from me," Ewing said. "They're willing to pay pretty good for a trail ride."

Jackson nodded. "What about anybody from his family?"

"What?" Ewing appeared not to understand the question.

"Cheston's family or friends, any of them ever come out here?"

Ewing narrowed his glance at the private detective. "Jackson, if I didn't know you were retired and recently in the hospital, I would think you're out here on business." His face hardened a bit. "What about it, Sister?"

Evangeline didn't know how to respond. "What about what, Mr. Ewing?"

"Your daddy here on business?" He smiled, but it seemed forced.

"Oh, you know the Captain, Mr. Ewing." She was trying to

lighten the mood. "Hard to let go of old habits. It's like he said—we were just on our way home from a doctor's visit and decided to stop by and say hello. We're sorry if we've interrupted you or made it sound like we were conducting a police interview."

The rancher dropped his shoulders, appearing to relax. "It's okay. I'm sorry. Just a little jumpy. I've had a lot of folks asking questions the last few weeks. I guess I'm oversensitive."

"No worries," Evangeline responded, taking over the conversation. "You about ready to head home?" she asked the Captain.

He didn't answer right away. He studied the rancher closely and then finally nodded. "You know, maybe I will try getting back on a horse again," he said.

Ewing seemed unsure of whether he was talking about right then or later. "Well, I think that's a nice idea. Maybe when it gets a little warmer, you can come over and get Aaron to ride out with you."

Evangeline clapped her hands together. "Let's head back to Madrid. I'm getting hungry." She turned to the rancher and held out her hand. "It was sure good to see you again, Mr. Ewing."

He nodded, taking her hand and giving it a squeeze. "Always a pleasure, Sister." He faced the Captain. "Jackson, you come any time you want to ride. I'm sure you'll find that you haven't lost a thing in being able to handle a horse." He patted his friend on the back as he turned to walk away.

"I'll give you a call," Jackson responded, and he headed down the porch steps.

Evangeline waved good-bye and joined the Captain. They both got into the truck and Eve started the engine.

"He's hiding something," was all the Captain had to say.

THIRTY-SEVEN

"And they all have alibis?" The Captain was sitting at his desk.

The cat was asleep on the cushion pushed into the corner behind him. Daisy was now a permanent resident of the private detective agency.

Evangeline was putting away some files in the cabinets located behind him in the back of the office.

"The son too?" He had spun his chair around and was facing Evangeline.

She turned to hear the rest of the phone conversation. She knew the Captain had asked a private detective in the Los Angeles area, a former FBI agent he knew from his days on the force, to check into the whereabouts of Cheston's family members during the time of the man's disappearance.

"Well, keep checking. Somebody out there has to know more than they're letting on." And he said a quick good-bye and hung up.

Evangeline waited a few seconds and then moved to the chair in front of the desk. She took a seat. "He didn't find out anything?"

Jackson shook his head. "There was a family trip that lasted a few days, including the day that Cheston was discovered to be missing. Wife, son, in-laws, even the family lawyer had all taken a long weekend to go up to the Santa Barbara area. It was somebody's wedding."

"And Cheston hadn't planned to attend with them?"

He scratched his chin. "JP . . ." He paused to explain. "My contact . . ."

And Evangeline nodded knowingly.

"He says the wife told him that Cheston hadn't planned to go. She said they'd rarely spent time together the last couple of years." He picked up a pen and started tapping it on the top of the desk. "She showed him a list of people who could vouch that she and the son were at the rehearsal party, the wedding, and the reception."

Evangeline listened. "Sounds like she was awfully eager to prove her innocence."

Jackson smiled. "JP thought the same thing. But I guess the family lawyer told her to have the alibi and the names of witnesses handy. He said she didn't seem to mind his questions, even after he explained he was working with a private detective in New Mexico. Of course, JP always had a way with the ladies. And from what he says, Mrs. Cheston was happy to have a male caller."

"Well, maybe if he's so good-looking, I should fly out to Los Angeles and get the full report in person." Evangeline grinned.

"You're a nun," the Captain reminded her. "And I wouldn't let J. P. Sanders get within twenty feet of either one of my girls."

"Wow," Evangeline responded. "Sounds like there's a story there."

Jackson waved away the comment. "There's no doubt JP's a charmer, but he's not to be trusted when it comes to women."

"I thought you two were friends."

"JP is a business contact. We were in the police academy together before he left to join the government. I respect his work. But I wouldn't call him a friend. And whatever you do, don't mention his name to Daniel."

"What did this guy do to Daniel?"

"The FBI and J. P. Sanders were brought in to New Mexico to work with the Santa Fe police on a high-profile drug-trafficking case. Daniel's wife served as a liaison between the force and the FBI. She and Sanders spent a lot of time together. Too much time, if you get my drift."

"Oh." Evangeline got the drift just fine. She remembered learning about Daniel's divorce when she was away at college, and even though she had never heard all the details, she'd heard enough to know Daniel had been devastated. "Then why would you call this guy?" she wanted to know.

"Because he's good at what he does. He gets answers faster than anybody I know."

"But he broke up your best friend's marriage."

"Like I said, don't tell Daniel."

Evangeline shook her head.

"What?" He seemed to sense her judgment.

"I just find it odd that you would keep in contact with a man who brought such turmoil into the life of your best friend."

"I don't keep in contact," he fired back. "I run into him from time to time at conferences and PI events."

"It just feels underhanded, deceptive," she responded.

"He's a good private detective, living in the area where I needed assistance. I asked him to carry out one assignment. He did that and I'll send him a check for his services. I'm not taking him out for dinner and dancing, for heaven's sake."

Eve shook her head. "I've just forgotten the ways of the world, I guess."

"What's that mean?"

"It just means I am used to honesty and truth-telling. I'm used to being in community with lots of people and working at authenticity in my relationships."

"That's a bunch of bull."

"Why would you say that? Why do you think it's a bunch of bull?"

"Because it is."

"How would you know?"

"Because I know people. And it doesn't matter if you live together in a gated community on a hill where you pray five times a day and take vows of poverty and chastity or whether you live thirty miles away from those you call friends and family, everybody hides things. Human beings by nature are just not truthful in how we represent ourselves, no matter who you're talking about." He stopped. "If one of the nuns fixes the oatmeal in the morning and it tastes like sawdust, and she asks, 'How's the oatmeal?' what do you tell her?"

Evangeline looked away. She thought it was a stupid analogy.

"You tell her it was fine oatmeal. Now, isn't that misrepresenting the truth?"

Evangeline's face reddened. "It's not the same thing as making a secret contact and a business arrangement with someone for your own gain when you know that contact and arrangement would be hurtful to someone you care about."

He retorted, "It's misrepresenting the truth in both aspects. And in the oatmeal scenario, there was an actual lie. In the arrangement I made with JP, an arrangement that was for one task with a beginning and an end, I haven't lied to anyone."

"I can't speak for anyone else, whether we're talking about those in the gated communities or those who claim to be in friendships. I can only speak for myself. And I seek to live my life in truthfulness. I am trying to be honest in all things. And I see your business arrangement with this man in Los Angeles and your need to keep it hidden from someone you claim is your friend as not being truthful, not honest." She looked away.

"And what about the reason you left Pecos?"

She jerked around to face him. "What are you talking about?"

"I'm talking about what you're really doing here."

She didn't reply.

"You've been away from the convent for almost a month now. I've got the prosthetic. In a couple of weeks I'll be released by the doctor to drive. Why haven't you called the vice superior and made arrangements to go back to the community? Why haven't you been honest instead of trying to make everyone else, including yourself, believe that the only reason you're here is to take care of me? I think you're enjoying working on this case a little too much. I think my surgery was a good excuse for you to get away from the monastery, maybe even away from your vows. I think there's something else going on with you, and you won't talk about it. And why haven't you gotten rid of that cat?" He spun around and pointed at the animal still asleep in the corner behind him. The cat looked up and yawned.

Eve glared at him. There were all kinds of things she wanted to say, truthful things, she thought, like telling him about the call she had with Dorisanne and why his other daughter wouldn't face him, things like he was a bully and how she thought her mother should have never stayed married to him. But she didn't say any of those things. Instead, Evangeline took in a breath and slowly exhaled. She made the decision to try to control her tongue. She would not speak in anger.

"When the doctor releases you to drive," she said, her voice calm, her tone remaining at a conversational level, "I will return to Pecos." She waited. "I'd like to help you pay some outstanding bills that I know you have, help you get the house set up in a way that you'll be comfortable living with your disability. I will take the cat with me. And I should be able to accomplish those things in the next couple of weeks while I'm still driving you. For now, I'm going home to fix us something to eat. When you're finished doing your paperwork or making your phone calls and want to come home for lunch, give me a call and I'll come back to get you."

And with that, she got up from her seat, picked up the truck keys from the desk, and walked away. The cat jumped up to join her. She slammed the door as she left, barely missing the exiting cat, walking at a cool, steady pace but feeling her heart pound.

THIRTY-EIGHT

———— ⟨❋⟩ ————

"What do you mean that he's suspicious?" Mother Madeline was fixing her guest a cup of tea. She was wearing a pink warm-up suit, white sneakers, and had her gray curly hair tied back with a pink bow.

Evangeline had never seen her mentor in such casual attire. She was used to seeing the older woman dressed from head to toe in black—a long black skirt, sensible black shoes, black jacket, black blouse, all serving as the background for the signature white priestly collar. It was surprising to see her in such bright clothes. She liked it and even wondered how it might be for her to add a little color to her casual wardrobe while she had one.

"He keeps asking me what I'm doing here, why I don't go back to Pecos for a morning service or afternoon meeting. He thinks I have some hidden agenda in taking the leave of absence." Evangeline leaned her elbows on her knees.

It was late in the morning and the sun was bright in the kitchen. The air was still. Spring was definitely upon them, and all the windows in the front area of the house were open. Madeline brought over a cup and set it before her friend.

"Thanks," Eve mumbled. She shook her head. "I leave my entire life behind to come take care of him, and he accuses me of not being honest, of hiding my true feelings." She took a sip of tea. "Well, I guess he's right about some of that, but I know if I let out some of my true feelings about him, we'd be in the same boat as he and Dorisanne."

Madeline took the seat across from Eve.

"He's just so cruel." Evangeline folded her arms across her chest. She closed her eyes, still trying to gather herself after the conversation she'd just had. "I understand he's having a difficult time with this setback. I know losing a leg has to be wrought with all kinds of feelings of loss and grief and frustration. He's worried about what will happen to him." Her eyes flew open. "But that doesn't mean he gets to take it all out on me. I do not deserve to be his punching bag."

Madeline nodded.

"I thought I had worked through all of this anger at him. I thought I had come so far with our relationship and my ability to take his abuse and not get hooked in to his criticisms and his need to incite those around him. I thought I had mastered this thing."

Madeline laughed, shaking her head. "Unfortunately, it takes more than just a few years in a convent to learn how to deal with family conflict."

"A few years? Madeline, I've been at the abbey for more than two decades! I'm forty years old. How much longer is it supposed to take?" She felt exasperated. "I have worked on issues of forgiveness, of acceptance, even of gratitude for the fact that he is responsible for my having life. But I don't think a human being should have to work their entire lifetime on trying to find a place of peace with a parent. At some point, I should be able to move on and focus on some other things."

"There are no other things," Madeline pointed out. "It's easy to say we're ready for loftier trials than figuring out how to have a conversation without getting our feelings hurt. That life is more than just negotiating household tasks and paying the bills. But these so-called little things are actually our best teachers. Our ability to connect in deeper and more meaningful relationships is developed only by living into these menial events. And if we continue to be stalled, even if it is always in just one relationship, we must work to understand those obstacles until they no longer impede our progress."

"I understand. But I just can't deal with him anymore," Evangeline confessed.

"Tell me, Eve," Madeline said, reaching out to touch her arm, "is there anything more to this? Could it be that his obstinacy and his ill temperament are just the net you've caught yourself in to keep from landing somewhere else?"

"I don't understand."

She pulled her hand away. "Okay," she replied without pressing.

"You think there's something else that I don't want to deal with? You think I'm using his bad behavior as a way to stop something else from surfacing?"

Madeline didn't answer. She drank from her cup of tea.

Evangeline sat back in her chair. "I guess it's not easy seeing your parents age," she commented.

Madeline shook her head. "No, not easy at all."

"And I suppose one can claim that they are prepared to take on the role of caregiver, but taking care of somebody else is not really all that easy." She smiled. "Even for one as spiritually mature as a nun."

"That's true too."

"What?" Evangeline could see Madeline had more on her mind.

"Those are possible reasons for your discontent," she replied.

"But you think there's more?" Evangeline sat up, leaned closer to Madeline. "You think he's right?"

Madeline lifted her eyebrows, her face a question mark. She finished her tea and set the cup back on the table. "Only you can answer that," she acknowledged.

Evangeline fell back in her chair.

Madeline got up from the table. "Would you like more tea?" she asked.

Evangeline looked in her cup. She had not drunk more than a few swallows. She shook her head.

The older woman placed her cup in the sink. She turned to face the table where Evangeline remained seated. "Why don't you tell me more about your father's murder case?"

Eve shrugged. She was not all that interested in recapping the information that had been gleaned since she last saw the retired priest.

"The man was here working on a new movie script?"

Eve thought for a moment. There'd been no discussion of Cheston's purpose for being in the area. She assumed that he was here for work, but maybe that needed to be asked of others. "I think so," she said. "I'm not sure I ever heard if he was perhaps the writer as well as the director of this new film that is supposed to be made here."

"The young woman was arrested?" Madeline pried.

Eve nodded. "She's out on bail, living in Santa Fe until the trial." She felt herself perk up a bit. The subject change did seem to improve her mood.

"Your father thinks she's innocent?"

Another nod.

"And you?"

"I don't think she's capable of murder," she answered. "I think she was really angry at the victim when they were last together, maybe even wanted him dead." She was holding her cup in both hands. "But no, I don't think she poisoned the man she loved and threw him off the side of a hill."

"There was an argument, then, between the victim and the accused?"

Evangeline nodded. "Apparently, he was mad at her for not trusting him to stay sober, and she was mad at him for not getting the divorce he had promised."

"Ah, the difficulties of love." Madeline turned and looked out her southward-facing window. "I guess you and I should be glad we have only to work so diligently on those relationships with family members and not those with lovers or spouses."

There was a sigh. "Right now, I think I'd prefer a lying, Hollywood-director boyfriend to a crotchety, old, one-legged father."

Madeline turned back to her guest and smiled. "I suppose it doesn't really matter who the others are that happen to be on our path walking with us. Mother, father, sister, boyfriend, roommate, we must still find a way to stumble forward together."

Evangeline put her cup to her lips and drank the tea she had been given and then wiped her mouth. "Either that or we kill 'em."

THIRTY-NINE

Evangeline rolled up the truck windows. The handles on both doors were old and not very secure, and she wrestled to get first one all the way up and then the other. She finally succeeded and fell back against the seat. It was warm enough to have them open but far too dusty. The winter snow had melted, and there had been no other precipitation for weeks. She put the truck in gear and drove along the bumpy dirt road, thinking about her conversation with Madeline as well as the one she'd had earlier that morning with the Captain. He always seemed to know just how to make her angry. Was he even aware of the way he pushed people's buttons?

"I guess it's just easier to pick on me instead of talking about how losing his leg makes him feel," she said out loud, recalling how he tried to antagonize her, how it almost felt like he wanted to make her mad so that maybe she'd leave or at least quit asking questions about how he was feeling.

Evangeline slowed the truck a bit as she pondered that idea. *Is he trying to push me out?* she wondered. *Is that what this is about?* Pushing her buttons certainly distracted her from asking anything more about his emotional and mental states. And making her mad was absolutely causing her to consider ending the leave of absence before the two months were up. Maybe that's all this was. Maybe he didn't really know more about her than she knew about herself. Maybe this didn't have anything at all to do with her need for serious soul-searching. Maybe he was just trying to get her out of his hair.

"Well, your methods are sure working!" she said as she snaked along the old mining road. As she slowly made a curve, the truck rattling as it moved across another cattle guard, she noticed the cabin situated on the far north side of the mesa. She drove beyond the gate she had already passed a number of times in the last few days and then stopped. She put the truck in reverse, swerved a bit to get off the road, and positioned the vehicle just below the entrance to Mr. Ross Biltmore's property. She yanked the truck into park and sat there for a few minutes before deciding that she would just take a brief look around. She turned off the engine, stuck the keys in her pocket, jumped out of the vehicle, glanced left and right, and headed to the gate.

It was exactly the way she had described it to the Captain, unlatched but chained. She looked around again and listened. She could hear nothing but a few trucks rolling down the highway that was more than five miles from where she stood. *No one should be coming out here today*, she thought, and she grabbed hold of the gate and climbed over it.

It was a longer walk to the cabin than she had expected. She wished she had worn her boots. Instead, since she'd thought she was only going over to visit with Madeline, she was wearing a pair of blue clogs she'd found in the back of her closet earlier that morning. She had figured they were Dorisanne's since she never remembered buying anything so fashionable, and even though they were comfortable when she put them on, trying to navigate a long walk was a bit more difficult than she had bargained for.

She noticed a path heading west from the driveway she was walking on and figured it was another old path that led either to the silver mine at Cedar Hill to the north or to some barn or storage facility on the property. She decided not to find out but rather to stick to the driveway that she was pretty sure led to the house on top of the mesa.

Soon she was standing next to the cabin, facing a long porch that extended along the east and south sides. She walked up, made note of what was there: rocking chairs; two fairly new, store-bought ones; an old bench; another old rocking chair beside it; and a stack of firewood in the corner. A red blanket was caught on a piece of the wood, and Evangeline guessed that it had been blown there by a recent spring wind. She figured it had flown off one of the rocking chairs or from the back of the bench. She glanced around once more and walked over and peeked in one of the windows.

The cabin had a large front room, a combination of a den and dining area. Thick, dark vigas lined the ceiling. There was a sofa, a couple of chairs, a leather recliner, all turned to face a kiva, an adobe-style fireplace, which appeared to have a new, smooth white finish. She could make out a small but ample kitchen, stainless-steel appliances, a long counter, and a hallway that she figured must lead to the back rooms, which probably included a sleeping area, a bathroom, maybe an office.

As she stepped away from the window and looked around the outside of the cabin, she suddenly remembered having been there before. It was very different than she recalled, had most certainly been remodeled: The interior added onto and opened up and a long, winding porch built around the exterior, but she was sure she had been on this property, in this cabin. And suddenly the memories all came back.

She had visited a boy who lived there with his family for the summer. She'd been only ten or eleven years old, and he had invited both Dorisanne and her to come over and go riding. His father was a rodeo cowboy and had a stable full of horses. There was also an outdoor riding arena, and this had been the place where Eve first heard about barrel racing. The boy's mother, also a rodeo regular, had shown Eve a few of the basics in how to ride for the event. Dorisanne had run off with the boy, Eve recalled, leaving her alone to receive an introduction to the sport she soon came to love. The family had not stayed in Madrid long, she thought. They had moved to Texas or Oklahoma, somewhere east; but that one visit had ignited a great passion. She started competing in barrel racing the following spring. The memories flooded her mind, and Eve couldn't help but smile thinking of how much she had loved the sport.

She walked around the cabin and looked through the window on the opposite side. From that point of view she could see a desk against the wall, with a typewriter and a stack of papers on top. And even though she doubted she would have the audacity to actually go into the house, she went ahead and gave the back door a try. She turned the knob. It was locked. She returned to the front, and as she headed around the corner, she noticed a sheet of paper lodged in the stack of wood, sticking out from beneath the red blanket. She pulled it out.

It was a page from a manuscript of some kind. It was typed, had a number centered at the bottom along with a title, *The Way of Broken Trails*. It was smudged and dirty and even ripped on one side. She figured it must have been there for some time, maybe as long as the owner of the house had been gone. She moved around to the north side of the house and leaned against the wall to read.

The page made little sense to Evangeline. It was part of a dialogue, what appeared to be a conversation between two men, one of them a law enforcement officer of some kind, the other a character in a jail or prison. It was simple, a bit of an argument or test of wills between the two. Trey and Hondo were the men's names; she could make that out from this one piece of the story, along with the title of the book, and that it was page 123. It also seemed as if they were discussing some past event, a former battle between the two over a girl. She couldn't get more than those few details.

She was starting to read it over again when she heard the sound of a vehicle approaching. She couldn't tell if it was a car or a truck, and she had no idea who was driving; she only knew that she was not supposed to be there. She slid down against the wall, clutching the piece of paper in her hands, hoping she would not be discovered.

FORTY

Eve stayed crouched against the wall, her heart racing. Her throat was dry, and she could feel beads of sweat forming along her top lip. She was not prepared to answer for her trespassing, and she didn't know how she could get away unnoticed. She closed her eyes and prayed. "Dear Lord," she whispered, "just get me out of here, and I won't do this again."

She heard a vehicle door open, and another, and then two male voices. She held her breath. *How will I explain what I'm doing here?* she wondered. And then she remembered the piece of paper in her hands. Would they think she was not only trespassing but also stealing? She quickly folded it up and stuck it in the back pocket of her pants. She waited, trying to hear who had driven up, hoping they might just knock on the front door and leave without discovering her.

Eve thought she heard them moving away and she rose up, considering the possibility that she could peek around the corner to see their whereabouts, maybe even make a run for it. Although with her sister's clogs and nothing to hide behind, she figured that might not be the best idea. She waited, but after hearing nothing and becoming much too curious, she remained in her crouched position and eased along the wall, inching over bit by bit. She had made it to the corner and was just about to slide around to look when she was face-to-face with a long, yellow snout and big, wet tongue.

"Trooper," she called out softly. "Go!" She tried to push the dog away. "Go on now," she commanded in a hushed whisper, to no avail.

The dog's tail was wagging so hard it beat loudly against the side of the house. Evangeline tried to move her aside and stop the noise, but it was too late. A set of mismatched legs stood right in front of her.

"Evangeline Louise Divine, what in the Sam Hill are you doing out here?"

She cleared her throat and stood up. "Hello, Captain," she said, forcing a fake smile.

"Jackson," a male voice was calling. "You all right? Is there somebody there?"

And before Eve could make a move or come up with an explanation for her hiding behind the house of a complete stranger, the Captain's former partner had joined him.

"Hello, Daniel," she said as a greeting. "It's nice today, don't you think?" She took in a big breath and dusted off the back of her pants. She felt the page sticking out and tried stuffing it in.

"Eve, what are you doing here?" her father repeated.

She still had the same big grin on her face. She cleared her throat, stalling. "Well, I was remembering that I came out here when I was a little girl, had my first barrel-racing lesson." She was thinking on her feet. "I rode below the house." She pointed behind them. "There used to be a full riding arena."

"You never came here," the Captain objected.

"I did once," she shot back. "I was ten or eleven. Mama brought me and Dorisanne to play with the little boy who lived here."

"Joseph Martinez never had any children," he responded, naming the man who had built the cabin and lived there for over forty years. "His wife died when she was young and he never remarried."

"Well, there was a summer when a family lived here, and the couple were rodeo riders, and they had a little boy with them," she explained, sounding like a child herself, a child who had just been caught breaking the rules by her father.

"The nephew," Jackson remembered. "Joseph had a nephew from Tennessee or Texas, and he and his wife lived here for about a year with the old man. It was right before he died."

"Exactly!"

"Rodeo riders," he added.

"Yes!" She sounded far too excited.

There was a pause.

"That still doesn't explain what you're doing here today," the Captain noted.

Eve scratched her head and looked around, trying to come up with a plausible explanation.

Trooper, not happy with being neglected, began dancing around her feet. She reached down and gave the dog a rub. "You have such a good nose!" she said. "Too good," she mumbled.

"Evangeline," Jackson called out. "Answer my question: What are you doing here?"

"Well, that's a good question," she finally stated. She brushed her hands on her pants, trying to shake the dog hair from them. "And what about you?" she asked, turning the question back on the two men.

"We got permission from Mr. Biltmore to see if there's anything out of place here," Daniel answered.

The Captain kept his eyes on Eve. "There've been reports of trespassing," he noted.

She raised her eyebrows. "My goodness . . ." was all she could think of to say. "In Madrid?" she asked innocently.

"Did you jump the gate?" he asked.

"I did," she replied. "Didn't know I still had it in me," she added. "It's a bit higher than I expected. And you?" she asked calmly.

"We cut the lock," he answered. "But like I said, we have permission from the property owner."

"You were able to reach Mr. Biltmore?" she asked. "In India?"

"We got a number for his hotel. Nice guy. He thought it was a good idea for us to come over and check things out," Daniel explained.

Evangeline grinned, shoving her hands into her pockets. She nodded. "Well, he'll be glad to know that it looks okay out here," she commented, as if she had been asked for a surveillance report. "I didn't see any evidence of a break-in or illegal passage."

"Except of course your own," the Captain said.

"Well, yes," she agreed. "Except my own."

Daniel watched the pair for a few seconds. "I'm going to take a look around out back," he advised. "You two going to be okay?"

"We're just fine," the Captain replied. "But maybe Eve can show us the property since she's so familiar with the place."

She shook her head. "Actually, I don't recall too much about the lay of the land," she answered, looking around.

"No?" the Captain asked. There was a note of sarcasm in his voice.

She shook her head. "The cabin is completely different from when I was here last. Did you notice the kitchen? And this great front porch? This was definitely not here when I visited." She motioned to the area around them. She felt like a real-estate agent trying to make a sale.

"Uh-huh," the Captain responded, unimpressed. He turned and followed Daniel as he headed around the house. "Why don't you just wait here until we get back." It was spoken as an instruction and not a question.

Eve closed her eyes, shook her head, and breathed a great sigh of relief.

FORTY-ONE

Jackson and Trooper rode back home with Evangeline, since she was parked outside the gate and Daniel needed to get to Santa Fe and file a report. It was well after the lunch hour, and Eve could feel her stomach rumbling. She remembered the earlier conversation in which she had told the Captain that she would be at home preparing the meal and that she would return to the office to pick him up. In all the talk they'd engaged in at the Biltmore property, they had not spoken of the noon meal or their most recent argument.

She turned on the vent. It was only early spring and not a record-temperature day, but since she had left the truck in the hot sun with the windows raised, the interior was quite warm when they got in. She switched the fan on high.

"You going to tell me what was going on back there?" The Captain opened his window and leaned his elbow on the frame. His other hand rested on the dog's back. Trooper sat between the two.

Eve kept her eyes on the road. "I had stopped by to see Madeline, and when I drove past the property, I just thought I'd look around." She shrugged. "Same as you, I guess."

"I'm investigating a murder," he said. "I had permission—"

She interrupted him. "From Mr. Biltmore, I know, you already told me. What connection did he have with Cheston anyway? Did you find that out?" She decided she wasn't going to try to explain her trespassing to him again.

She could feel him watching her. She turned and faced him.

"They were college roommates," he answered.

She nodded. "I'm guessing that was a long time ago."

"Thirty years," he noted. "Did you discover anything interesting before we arrived?" It appeared as if he was going to let her have her way. No more questions about why she had parked outside somebody's locked gate, jumped it, and hid behind the house.

She reached into her back pocket and pulled out the page she had found. She handed it to him.

The Captain unfolded the paper. He studied his daughter. "Where did you get this?"

"On the stack of wood on the front porch." She waited. "In the corner. It had gotten caught there. Must have been lost or misplaced or thrown out. I don't know."

He glanced down at the paper. "What is it?"

"A page from a manuscript or screenplay, I'd say. Looks like the title is *The Way of Broken Trails*."

He appeared to be reading.

"Mr. Biltmore is a writer, right?" she asked.

"That's what Daniel said," the Captain answered.

"Then I guess this is his."

"I guess," he responded.

"We can google the title and see if it's a published book or screenplay that's been sold. I don't think I've ever heard of it." She paused. "You?"

He shook his head. "But then I don't get out much to bookstores or the movies." He folded the page back up and stuck it in his front shirt pocket. "I feel like I may have mishandled things earlier."

She turned to look at him. "What?"

"At the office," he explained. And he cleared his throat.

She didn't know how to respond. She wasn't sure what he was saying. Was this an apology?

"It's none of my business why you left the convent. You're a grown woman, and you can make your own decisions. The fact that you've been here with me has been very helpful, and I was wrong to question your motives. You are welcome to stay as long as you like."

She stared at the road in front of them. She couldn't even think of a response. *He must have explained what happened to Daniel,* she thought. He wouldn't have thought to say this without some advice, and this sounded exactly like something his friend would have told him to say.

"But you can't go trespassing on other people's property anymore," he instructed. "It's bad for business. And you need to slow down."

"Got it," she replied, letting off the gas, still stunned by his comments.

The two rode in silence as the dirt road ended at the highway. Eve signaled to turn toward home. Before she pulled out, she glanced ahead of her and noticed the house situated a few hundred yards off the road. "Does Miss Buttercup still live over there?" She pointed in the direction of the property in front of them.

"Who?" He didn't recognize the name.

"Miss Buttercup," she repeated herself. "That's what we called her because she always wore a yellow bonnet. Dorisanne said she looked like a flower. We called her Miss Buttercup."

"The librarian?"

"That's her," she replied.

"Her name is LuEllen Blanchard." He looked at Eve. "How come I never knew you called her that?"

"There are a whole lot of names Dorisanne and I gave people in Madrid that you don't know about." She still hadn't pulled out from the intersection.

"The Captain, I know about that one."

Eve didn't know what to say. Even though their mother had tried to make the two girls quit calling him by that title, he had never acted like he minded. At least, he never ordered them to stop.

"Does she still live there?" she asked again, ignoring his comment.

"She does," he answered, and then he slowly began to under-stand what his daughter was thinking.

They both knew that the victim's BMW had been located on a mining path off the dirt road they were on, the one that ended right in front of the librarian's house.

"It is possible that she might have taken notice of the recent traffic on this particular stretch of road," he said.

"It wouldn't hurt to stop and just see, do you think?" She looked left and right. No cars were coming in either direction.

"Wouldn't hurt a thing," he replied. "Except your stomach. I can hear it growling over here. I had a pack of crackers about ten o'clock when I took my insulin. I suspect you haven't had anything since breakfast."

"I can wait a bit longer," she said, and headed across the highway and into the driveway that stopped beside the little house.

FORTY-TWO

Eve put the truck in park. When she got out, the Captain had already exited the vehicle and was standing in front of her. The speed with which he had moved surprised her. He was adapting to the prosthetic without too much trouble. She'd thought the same thing when she watched him walking up the path with Daniel at the Biltmore property. There was a slight limp, the tiniest change to his gait, a minor lean on his good leg, and a little difference in the size, but other than that, a person would have a hard time knowing he even had an artificial limb. *He was doing really well*, she thought.

She followed him as he headed up the front walk to the house. When she joined him at the door, he rang the bell. In a few minutes the door opened, and a large, older woman was facing the father and daughter. She was wearing a bright yellow dress and a big grin.

"Captain Divine," she said. "I thought that was your truck." She had a dish towel in her hands and was wiping them. "And Sister Eve." She threw the towel across her shoulder and reached out.

Evangeline took one of the extended hands and squeezed it. "Miss Blanchard," she said and smiled. "We were just out for a morning drive, and we thought we would drop in and say hello."

"Well, isn't that a treat for me? Won't you come in?" And she moved aside, making room for the two to enter.

The house felt cool as Evangeline and the Captain stepped inside. Eve could not remember ever being there before, and as she looked around, it was easy to see the older woman had a love for the written word. There were books stacked everywhere, including on the sofa, which looked like the only place guests might sit. There were shelves and tables but no other chairs in the room.

"Let's go into the kitchen," the woman said, heading into the next room. "I'm sorting through all my collections and I'm afraid I've made a huge mess."

The two followed behind her, saw that there were even more books in the other room, and waited as she cleared a place for them to sit at the table.

"Can I get you something to drink?" she asked.

"I would love some water," Eve answered.

"Captain?"

"No, no, I'm fine," he replied.

The woman poured the drink for Eve and headed back to the dining table. She handed it to her guest and squeezed her on the shoulder. "You and your sister used to come to the library every Saturday morning," she said.

Eve took a long swallow. She was very thirsty. She wiped her mouth. "We did," she said. "And you always had the books on our list pulled and ready for us."

"*A Wrinkle in Time*," she noted, taking her place at the table. "You loved Madeleine L'Engle."

"Still do," Evangeline agreed.

"You were always bringing in migrant children, trying to get them library cards, even the ones without proper addresses."

The woman turned to her other guest before Eve could respond. "And, Captain, how are you doing since the operation?" She shook her head and made a kind of clucking sound. "Diabetes can wreak such havoc on a body."

He nodded. "I'm doing just fine," he replied.

"I am so glad to hear it."

"So, Miss Blanchard, how long have you been retired?" Eve wanted to know. She drank another swallow of her water.

"Let's see. I think it's been eight years now," she said. "A glorious eight years," she added.

Eve nodded. "And how are things at our little county library?"

"We have a fabulous young lady from Albuquerque working there, and we've added computers and a Tuesday evening book club. I still volunteer there two mornings a week, but I am very happy not to be bothered with budget cuts and electronic books." She sighed. "But pleasantries aside"—she slid a strand of gray hair behind her ear—"I'm sure you didn't drop by to hear me mourn the passing of leather-bound classics. What you really want to know is whether or not I saw a certain BMW pass my way."

Jackson quickly turned to Evangeline, and the two then faced the woman.

"Jackson Divine, you're easier to read than a picture book."

FORTY-THREE

—◦✳❉✳◦—

"Well, that was helpful, don't you think?" Evangeline was in the kitchen heating up some soup. She had made sandwiches but had already eaten half of hers while preparing the rest of the meal. It was well after two o'clock, and she couldn't help herself, she was famished.

Jackson was seated at the table. He had a laptop computer open and was preoccupied searching for more information about Ross Biltmore and a book or screenplay titled *The Way of Broken Trails*. He mumbled a reply.

"I mean, how is it that no one thought to stop and ask her if she had seen anything when Cheston went missing? It seems so obvious to me that with the view of the dirt road from her house, she could be a very important witness."

He still didn't reply. He was typing and reading.

"She was certainly clear that she had seen the BMW driving up that road a number of times, even if she didn't see it the day he disappeared. That now makes two witnesses who know Cheston drove on that road, and it seems very likely that he was visiting his old college roommate. There's nothing else up there except Madeline's house and the mines."

There was no response.

She poured the soup into two bowls and placed the pan in the sink. "And then to remember seeing a black SUV racing from the west end to the intersection on the morning Cheston disappeared, and then speeding away so quickly, well, that has to tell us something. And the fact that she remembers it had a California license plate, that's incredible!"

She walked to the table and placed the bowls down. She leaned against the chair where she was accustomed to sitting at meals. "Cheston must have gone to Biltmore's house that morning before dawn, and somebody was either following him or was there waiting." She studied the Captain, thinking. "Then the driver of that SUV killed Cheston, drove his BMW up past the mine, walked back to Biltmore's, and drove down the dirt road and out of town. Miss Buttercup saw the getaway."

She slapped the back of the chair and the Captain, startled, jerked his head in her direction. He stared at her.

She continued, "And she said that the vehicle headed north, going away from Madrid. If Megan was in that car and needed to hurry back to the house before the airport driver arrived, she would have turned left. The house where they were staying was left, not right. This gives us proof that Megan wasn't the killer."

The Captain studied her. "That's a stretch, don't you think?"

"I don't see it that way," she replied, taking her seat.

Jackson shook his head. "We don't know that Cheston was on that road the day he disappeared. She didn't see him drive out there. Nobody saw him drive out there. And that SUV could have been anybody. It could have been a tourist from California who got lost and was in a hurry to find their way. All she saw was a car coming out from the direction of Biltmore's house. She didn't see it driving up there, so we don't even know how long it had been up that road. It could have been someone camping at the mines the night before. You know how folks love to poke around up there."

Eve nodded. He was right. She bowed her head, finished her prayer, and started eating her soup. She contemplated the new information they had just received. All that Miss Buttercup had really given them was the fact that she had seen Cheston's car heading up the dirt road that went to Mr. Biltmore's property a couple of times before he disappeared. She had only confirmed what they had already suspected after hearing Mother Madeline say she had seen the car in Biltmore's driveway once herself. She took a bite of her sandwich. All they really knew was that Cheston had visited his old college roommate.

"But this is interesting."

"What?" she asked.

The Captain turned the laptop around so that Eve could see the screen.

It was an article announcing the production of a film being directed by Charles Cheston. The source was the *Hollywood Reporter*, and it had been published about six months earlier. It listed the names of the director, Cheston; the producer, Polland; the stars, Megan Flint and the latest Hollywood hunk whose name

Eve didn't recognize; the location, central New Mexico; and the title, *The Way of Broken Trails*. There was a short description of the movie as a Western with a bit of science-fiction flair, and the article also mentioned the name of the screenwriter. Eve glanced up at Jackson. He was grinning. The name was the same as the film's director, Charles Cheston.

FORTY-FOUR

⸻ ✳✳✳ ⸻

She took a spoonful of soup, swallowed, and dabbed at the corners of her mouth. She was trying to follow where the Captain was taking this.

He read her confusion. "Maybe Cheston lied about being the writer. Maybe he got his material from Biltmore," Jackson guessed. "Maybe that's the reason he was in town, that's the reason for the visits up that dirt road and onto the driveway of his friend's property."

He didn't wait for a response. He turned the laptop back around. He pulled down the top a ways and slid it over, making room for his soup and sandwich. "And maybe that's the reason you found a sheet of paper with this title on it at Biltmore's house." He took a spoonful of soup, chewed the piece of chicken that had landed in his spoon, and swallowed. "Cheston had a ghostwriter."

Evangeline ate the rest of her sandwich. "And maybe Biltmore wasn't happy that he didn't get the credit for writing."

Jackson continued eating and shrugged. "It could be a business deal that went south. Biltmore could have blackmailed Cheston for more money, or maybe he wanted his name in lights along with that of his buddy and Cheston said no. Or maybe Cheston just outright stole the book and Biltmore found out."

"But Ross Biltmore was out of town when Cheston disappeared. We know that he was on a flight to India a couple of days before Megan declared that he was missing." She shook her head. "It doesn't sound like he could be a real suspect in the murder."

"He could have hired someone to take care of the dirty business." The Captain was enjoying his lunch. "That could have been the driver of the SUV."

"I don't know," she responded. "That seems awfully hard to prove." She wiped her mouth. "You'd have to get Mr. Biltmore to come back, and he certainly isn't going to do that unless he's charged and extradited by the police. Since they're happy with the suspect they have, I don't see them making those arrangements."

Jackson nodded. "I thought about that," he noted. "But what if I make a call to him and, let's say, just roll out this idea of Cheston stealing his work, and see what kind of response we get? At least we would know if there was motive. We'd be able to tell if he was unhappy with his old friend or if this was a business relationship of some sort." He continued to eat.

Eve nodded. It was all making sense to her. She loved where the work was taking her, the thoughts, the possibilities. She was excited about where the Captain was going. "Do you have the number of where he's staying in India?"

He reached into his pants pocket and pulled out a slip of paper.

"Daniel gave it to me when he came this morning to let me know he had gotten permission to check out the property." He smiled.

"I thought of something else."

Jackson put the slip of paper on the table and listened.

"Did anybody ever check out the drug connections Cheston had?" Evangeline had wondered if Megan had been right and that he was sober and clean when she arrived, or maybe he was just very good at hiding it. "It's like that part of his life is completely being overlooked."

Jackson finished off his sandwich. He seemed to be thinking about the question. "I don't know the answer to that." He took a drink from his glass of milk. "But I think that's also worth some of our time."

"I could make a visit to Megan in Santa Fe. I sort of wanted to see her anyway. I know this must be a very tough time for her. House arrest has to be terrible," she said. "She talked to me while you were in the hospital, shared some things, some confidential things."

"She made a confession?" the Captain wanted to know.

Eve shrugged. "Something like that." She wasn't going to tell anything more about the intimate conversations she had with Megan. "Anyway, maybe she can shed some light on where Cheston bought his drugs. She certainly knew a lot about his drug habits. Maybe she could help us out with some names."

Jackson agreed. "Wonder what time it is in India."

"Look it up online maybe?"

He nodded, opened the laptop back up, and typed in something. Eve waited.

"Looks like it's too early to be making a call. I'll wait until tonight."

Eve nodded. She was impressed that he seemed to know so much about the computer. His skills were certainly more expansive than hers. She kept up with the abbey's website and could make a spreadsheet and send and receive e-mails, but she wasn't very savvy about the latest technology.

"I need to take my insulin," Jackson said. "But I'd sort of like to take a little trip into town myself. There's something Daniel told me about Polland that I want to check out."

"You want to go to the station?" Eve asked, surprised. She knew her father had been pushed out of the loop since taking the case on Megan's behalf. Daniel sneaking him information was one thing, but to just show up at the station to ask a question was an entirely different approach.

"They can't stop a retired man from checking on his pension payments." And he finished the last of his soup, patted his stomach to show he was satisfied, and pushed himself away from the table.

FORTY-FIVE

Once Evangeline was cleared by the officer posted at the front door of the place where Megan was staying under house arrest, she headed inside. She could hear music playing in one of the rooms. Someone, Megan she presumed, was singing along loudly. She stood at the door calling out the young woman's name. Finally, the music was turned off and Megan came walking toward her from the back of the house.

"Sister Evangeline!" she shouted and quickly ran to Eve and grabbed her in a huge embrace. "I am so glad to see you!"

Eve was startled by the grand show of affection. She was also almost knocked down by the petite star. "Well, I am glad to see you too," she said, steadying herself.

"Come in, take off your coat. Would you like tea? I have tea." She ushered Eve into a sitting area, tugging off her coat as she entered. She took the garment and walked back out into the hallway, to hang it up, Eve guessed.

The room was large and decorated tastefully in southwestern charm. There were shelves filled with Indian pots, drums, and kachina dolls, dark leather furniture, tan walls, and ceramic tile flooring. There was a kiva fireplace and beautiful artwork throughout. If the rest of the house looked like this, Eve thought, Megan wasn't in as bad a shape as she first expected. This was certainly better than any house arrest she could imagine.

"Should I build a fire?" she asked. "And what about the tea? Did you say you wanted tea?"

Eve shook her head and held out her hand. "Megan, it's okay. Calm down. Let's just sit and talk."

Megan nodded and pulled Eve over to the sofa. The two sat down. The young woman immediately pulled her legs up under her so that she was sitting on them. She bounced a little and Eve thought something seemed very odd about her hostess.

"Megan, are you all right?" she asked.

The young woman leaned up and then fell back against the cushions. "Who, me?" she asked. She shook her head, grabbed a pillow, and hugged it. "I'm great! I've got this great house and all these old movies to watch. There's a karaoke machine. I can talk on the phone and have a massage once a day, get my nails done. I'm just great." She shot her legs out and bounced some more.

"Are you staying here alone?"

"Who, me?" She placed the pillow that had been in her arms between her and Eve and picked up another. "I am, mostly. Ron—" She stopped. "Mr. Polland, he comes and stays some with me. And there's David outside, no, wait . . ." She jumped up and ran to the window and looked out. "No, that's Billy out there right now."

She flew back to her place on the sofa. "One of them is always out there if I need something. They're both really nice." She pulled her legs in and sat cross-legged. She grinned at Eve. "But I'm so glad to see you. I thought you might be gone back to the convent and I wouldn't see you again."

Eve shook her head. She narrowed her eyes at Megan, trying to figure out what was going on. She was talking so fast, moving so much.

"Megan, did you take something this morning?"

Megan fell back laughing. "I did!" she answered. "Ron gave me some pills to help me, you know, feel better." She pulled the pillow close and dropped her face into it. "I was so depressed," she added.

Eve was at a loss. Clearly, Megan was on something that was making her absolutely manic.

"Did you hear that?" Megan asked and jumped up again, running to the window. "It's the mailman. Or the mail lady. I'm not really sure." She turned to Eve. "I can always hear when they come. The mail is dropped through a slot in the door. You want to see?" And she ran from the room. There was a scream, and Eve was just about to get up and see what had happened when Megan flew back into the room.

"I have a letter!" she yelled and threw herself back on the sofa.

Eve reached out her hand, taking Megan by the arm. "What kind of pills did Ron give you, Meg?"

She laughed. "Orange ones," she replied. "Like little sunshines. And they really make me feel so happy." She held the letter in her hands and raised her arms over her head. "I was sad before I took them. I miss Chaz," she said. "I miss being with him. I miss feeling like I was special." And she fell into Eve's arms.

"I know you do, Megan." And she patted her on the back while the young woman buried her head in Eve's shoulder.

She jerked back. "You don't think I killed him, do you, Sister?"

Evangeline shook her head. "No, Megan, I don't think you killed Charles."

"Because everybody else does," she said, her voice sounding like a child's. She slumped back into the sofa.

"Who else does?" Eve asked.

"That mean ex-wife of his, for one. She's telling everybody that I killed him because I was jealous of her." She grabbed the pillow she had been holding earlier, pulling it close to her chest. She turned to Eve. "I'm not jealous of her," she said.

"I know, Megan."

"And then there's that awful son of his, Charles Jr., CJ," she said sarcastically. "He wrote some terrible things on Facebook, called me awful names." She dropped her head into the pillow. "I'm not awful," she said, her words sounding smothered.

"I know, I know," Eve said, trying to comfort her.

"Even Ron thinks I did it." She looked up. "He hasn't said it, but I know he thinks that." She started to cry, dropping her head back into the pillow.

"Why would Ron think you killed Chaz?" Eve asked.

"Because I was really mad," she confessed.

"Because you thought he was using drugs again?"

She shook her head with her face still in the pillow.

"Because he wouldn't divorce his wife?"

She lifted up and faced Evangeline. "I knew he wasn't going to leave her."

"Then why were you really mad?"

Megan punched the pillow.

"Because he had promised another girl that she could have my part in the movie." She punched it again and then fell to the side, pulling the pillow on top of her.

"How did you find that out?" Eve wanted to know.

"She called the house in L.A. and left a message," she answered, the words muffled by the pillow. "I heard what that girl said about being so happy to read the script and to have the role." She sat up, still clutching the pillow, and shook her head. "Betsy Wetsy . . . My mom told me about Betsy Wetsy dolls. I always thought that was such a funny name. *Betsy Wetsy*. Did you have a Betsy Wetsy doll, Sister Eve?"

Eve looked around for a box of tissues. With all that crying, Megan was in real need of wiping her nose. "I didn't have many dolls, Megan. I liked to play with cars and trucks when I was little."

"Oh," Megan replied.

"Did you like dolls?" Eve asked.

"Yes. I liked dolls. But I didn't have a Betsy Wetsy doll." She bit her bottom lip. "Anyway, what was I talking about?" She squinted her eyes together, her face pinched in a knot, trying to stay on topic. "Oh, right," she exclaimed. "The girl on the phone. Betsy. She wanted to read for the role. Yeah, that's right. But I fixed that!" she said. "I called Betsy Wetsy and told her I had that part and she was not getting it. I told her he was only lying to her and that he was in New Mexico writing the ending for me, not for her, for me!" She slid her arm under her nose. "And then I flew down here to let Chaz have it."

No need for a handkerchief now, Evangeline thought. "Okay, okay, Megan." She rubbed the young woman's back. "Let me get you a cup of tea." She eased out of her seat. "You just stay there and let me fix it for you, okay?"

Megan nodded dutifully. "But I didn't kill him," she whimpered.

Eve headed into the kitchen, filled the teapot, and began searching for some tea. She found a variety of bags in a canister near the stove. She chose chamomile, hoping it might provide a calming effect. She didn't know what kind of drugs Polland was feeding Megan, but she knew she was going to have to put a stop to it. Seeing Megan so strung out frightened her, and she was concerned that when the trial began, if there was one, a drug habit might only get worse.

She waited for the teapot to whistle, poured the water into the cup over the bag, and headed back into the sitting room. She was smiling. "Here's a nice cup of tea. Maybe this will help calm you down a bit, Megan."

Eve looked down at the sofa, holding out the cup. Megan lay fast asleep.

FORTY-SIX

—————— ⋅✳⋅✳⋅✳⋅ ——————

"Why is he giving her Adderall?" the Captain wanted to know. "And would you please slow down?"

Evangeline was taking the ramp from St. Francis Street to Highway 25. They were heading back to Madrid. She sighed and took her foot off the gas, slowing the truck.

"I don't know." She signaled and carefully merged onto the highway. She shook her head. "She couldn't tell me. She was totally out of it. And quit complaining about my driving. You were the one who taught me."

"I didn't teach you to speed," he replied. "Did you contact Polland?"

Eve nodded. "I got Megan into bed, and I found his number and made the call. He was back in L.A."

"What did you say?"

"That drugging Megan was not the best way to help her through this difficult time." She picked up speed and then thought better of it. She slowed down.

"And how did he take that?"

"Actually, he sounded quite gracious and concerned. He said that he got the prescription from Megan's doctor, and they had both agreed that taking one or two of the pills a day might help her through this." She fiddled with the rearview mirror. "He said that he hadn't seen how she reacted to the medication, and now that he had heard this from me, he would definitely not let her take any more. We made arrangements for a nurse to be with her until he gets into town. He said he was returning tonight."

"Did you get rid of what was there?" Jackson was rubbing the spot beneath his knee where the prosthetic was attached.

"I flushed them," she answered, noticing his actions. "Your leg sore?"

He stopped rubbing it. "Nah, just a habit."

She watched him from the corner of her eye. She could tell he was lying.

"So, I guess you couldn't ask her anything about where Cheston got his drugs?"

She shook her head. "It was a wasted visit in that aspect." She turned on her signal, heading in the direction of Highway 14. "She could only tell me how everybody thinks she's the murderer. Charles's family is apparently making use of the television and Internet coverage. I guess she reads and hears it all."

"You'd think Polland would know to protect her from all that," Jackson groused.

"What about your visit?" she wanted to know. "How did things go at the police station?"

"Painter wasn't too happy to see me," he reported and grinned. "He couldn't toss me out, though, because my old friends in

Human Resources backed up my claim that I was there to find out about my pension."

Eve laughed.

"He was so mad he left. He told his assistant that he was going over to the capitol building because he had an appointment with the governor." He rolled his head around, giving his neck a few good stretches. "He loves making himself sound important."

"So, you had time to see some folks, ask some questions, read a few reports?" She pulled down her visor and sat back in the driver's seat.

"Hinds was out, too, so yes . . ." He nodded. "I heard most of what they've got."

"And?"

"And they know Megan was with Cheston the night he disappeared. They know he was driving a BMW while he stayed in Madrid and that his prints were found in the car, but there were no bloodstains or anybody else's DNA. They still haven't located his cell phone or laptop computer. Everybody in the family is cleared. Polland raised their suspicions a bit because of how he hovers over Megan, wasn't that happy with his star director, and because he doesn't have an alibi for the night. He claims he was home watching dailies." He turned to Eve. "That's movie talk for scenes shot but not yet edited."

She nodded. "Gotcha."

"He had been scheduled to make an appearance at some charity event, but he backed out at the last minute."

"To watch dailies," Eve added.

"That's what he says."

"I don't really get it. Even if he doesn't have anybody to say he was where he said he was, why is he a suspect? Didn't he need Cheston alive to make this film? Wasn't Cheston the golden calf of Polland Productions?"

"That's where it gets interesting," Jackson replied.

"Tell me," Eve responded. She couldn't help it, she was excited.

"Well, Polland had given Cheston a lot of money in advance for writing the film. He says Cheston came to him a couple of months before he disappeared and told him that all the money was gone. The director was asking for more."

"Did he give it to him?"

The Captain shook his head. "He says he told Cheston that he couldn't have any more money until they started production."

"I guess Charles wasn't too happy about that," Eve surmised.

"No, I guess not. And it sounds like Polland thought Cheston was stealing from him."

"How would that have been possible?" Eve asked.

"I'm not so sure about that."

"And the meeting Cheston was scheduled to have in L.A. the day he disappeared, what was that about?"

"Polland told the detective that the meetings arranged on the day he disappeared were meant to put the final script in the producer's hands and to prove to the investors that Cheston and this script were worth all the trouble."

"And Cheston agreed? He said yes to the meeting and told them that the script was finished?" Eve asked.

Jackson nodded while Eve thought about whether Polland could be telling the truth about the film and the meeting and the script.

"This script that everybody knows about, has anybody actually seen it?" Eve was still curious about the college roommate and his involvement, if any, in writing the screenplay.

"Not the last act or scenes or whatever they call it," Jackson answered and then yawned. He rubbed his eyes. "Most of the script had been read and approved, but Polland claims that he had still not seen the ending. That was why Cheston was in New Mexico. He told everyone he was finishing the script, and he told Polland that he needed to be on location to work out the ending." He sighed. "What we don't know is whether Polland is lying. Maybe he already had the last pages and killed the director because he was done with him, or maybe he got tired of waiting on Cheston and found someone else who could finish it. Maybe he found out Cheston was stealing from him, and he drove down to Madrid in his black SUV, confronted Cheston, they had a fight, and he killed him. And maybe he's hovering like a concerned friend and even feeding Megan drugs to cover up the fact that he's really letting her take the fall."

Eve considered this possible scenario. "But Megan called Polland when Cheston didn't show up. If he was driving back to L.A., how would she have contacted him?"

Jackson looked at Eve. "How did you call him today?"

She nodded, understanding where he was going with the question. "On his cell."

The Captain shrugged. "He could have been anywhere and taken the call, acted upset, and told Megan and the pilot to come back and hunt for Cheston, all while he was driving as fast as he could to get back to California before anybody noticed he had gone out of town."

"Something else." She tapped a finger on the steering wheel. "If Cheston was really finishing the script and planning to bring it to the meeting, there had to be some proof of that in the house. Did anybody ever find any evidence that he had been writing?" She figured there should have been an office, a desk, a home computer, pages, something to show his work at the house he had rented.

Jackson shook his head. "There were copies of the unfinished script that Polland and the others had seen. But there were no new pages or any evidence of writing being done anywhere at the house or in L.A. But Megan said he never worked on a desktop computer anyway, only on the laptop."

"And that's still nowhere to be found." Eve recalled that bit of information.

Jackson leaned against the headrest and grew quiet.

Eve glanced over and could see he had closed his eyes. Deciding not to engage him in any more conversation, she took advantage of her father's rest, pressed the gas pedal, and hurried home.

FORTY-SEVEN

———— ✦✦✦ ————

"Is it infected?" Evangeline had closed the door to the Captain's room and was following the nurse up the hall to the kitchen. "He's not been letting me look at it since he's gotten the prosthetic. When I saw it this morning, I knew it wasn't good."

The nurse stopped at the kitchen counter and waited for Eve to join her.

"I thought he was doing so well. Yesterday, he was up all day. He went to Santa Fe, seemed to be feeling great." She walked past the nurse and stood beside the table. She suddenly recalled his nap in the truck on the way home, the way he kept rubbing his leg. She should have realized then, she thought.

"He is doing fine," the nurse replied. "His blood sugar readings have been normal every time I've checked." She stopped. "Although it is a little high right now, so I gave him a shot of insulin. I think it's time, right?"

Eve glanced at the clock. She nodded.

"Good. His blood pressure is normal, pulse is great." She gave an encouraging smile. "All in all he has done very well since the amputation, much better than most of my patients once they're home from the hospital."

"But an infection in his leg, that's not good. That's what led to the surgery in the first place, right, an infection in his foot that wouldn't clear up?" Eve pulled out a chair and sat down at the table.

"That was a really bad wound, and it had been infected a long time. This sore doesn't look that bad. It may not even be infected, just a little raw from the prosthetic rubbing it. By using ice and getting more rest, extending his antibiotics for a couple more weeks, I think this will clear up. And he can still use the crutches. He doesn't have to stay in bed."

"He can't wear the prosthetic, though, can he?" Eve looked at the nurse.

She shook her head. "No, he'll need to be off the leg for a week or so. And I'll talk to the prosthetist and see if we can find a way to keep the top strap from digging into his skin. I'm sure this happens all the time. It just takes awhile for the stump to heal and then awhile for the fit to be just right. I've heard patients say it was a year or more before they felt comfortable using the artificial limb. I'm pretty sure your father pushed things a little too fast."

The nurse walked around to the other side of the kitchen counter where she had left her files, her tote bag still on the barstool. She pulled out a file and made a few notes in a chart and then reached into her bag, rifled through the papers, and pulled a piece from another file and handed it to Evangeline.

"This tells you what signs to look for that might indicate the sore has become infected—more redness, swelling, hot to the touch anywhere around the bottom of the stump, a fever, blood sugar above 250, delusional or irrational behavior. If any of those things happen, call 911 and get him to the hospital."

Eve glanced up. "Irrational behavior? You mean like he suddenly becomes kindhearted and sweet and says 'Thank you' and 'Please' and doesn't fuss when you tell him he can't have things his way?"

The nurse laughed. She gathered up her belongings. "Exactly."

Eve smiled. She stood up from her seat. "Would you like a bottle of water or a piece of fruit to take with you to your next appointment?"

The nurse shook her head. "No, but thanks for offering. I'll be heading to the office once I leave, and I have something waiting for me there."

"Okay," Eve responded. She walked over to the door and opened it. "Thank you so much for coming when I called."

She turned and squeezed Eve on the arm. "Any time, Sister," she said and headed out the door and down the front steps. "He's really lucky you were able to get time away from the convent and be here with him."

Eve forced a smile. She watched as the nurse waved and got into her car and drove away. She closed the door, glanced in the direction of the back of the house, and sighed. With everything heating up with Megan's case, she knew the Captain would think the same thing she was thinking: This was not the best time for a setback.

FORTY-EIGHT

———— ❊❊❊ ————

"One of us has to go to Los Angeles." The Captain was sitting up in his bed. He had spent the morning at the office trying to run down a few facts, including the exact time that Ross Biltmore would be arriving at the Albuquerque airport the following day. "One of us has to stay here and talk to Biltmore, and one of us has to go to L.A. and check out the house Megan and Cheston shared, see if there's anything there that can help out her case."

"I thought you had the creepy guy working for you in L.A." Evangeline knew the only one with the ability to ask the right questions and get the necessary information from Ross Biltmore was the Captain. She was trying to figure out alternatives to handle the situation.

"JP?" he asked.

"Yeah, wife-thieving, creepy guy," she replied. She was sitting in the chair opposite the bed. After watching him grimace every time he moved, she had told the Captain that if he didn't rest for an hour, she was going to call their neighbor with the funny-smelling car, Delphine, to come over for a visit and then leave her there while she went back to the office. It was a surprise to Eve, but he had complied and headed to his room to take a nap. She wasn't sure if he was as tired as he appeared or if the threat actually worked.

"What do you know about wife-thieving, creepy guys?" he asked.

"You think because I'm a nun I don't know about wife-thieving, creepy guys?" she asked.

"I think because you're a nun you're not supposed to call them that."

"Call them what?"

"Wife-thieving, creepy guys."

"Oh."

There was a pause. She decided to let that thread of the conversation go. "So, what happened to JP?"

"I decided not to use him anymore," he said. He fluffed up the pillows behind his head. "And don't go thinking it had anything to do with your little sermon on truth-telling or friendship."

Evangeline couldn't help grinning.

"One of us has to go to L.A., and since you don't trust your instincts in getting any details out of our world-traveling writer about his relationship with Cheston and you want me to handle that, I think that narrows it down to you. You need to go to Los Angeles and check out things in the house Megan shared with him, see if there's anything in his personal effects that might give us some clue that he had been writing this script or that there was a business arrangement with Biltmore. See if there's a computer and check the files, although I imagine the police took that with the search warrant."

Eve wasn't prepared for such an unexpected assignment, but she was starting to like the idea of a trip. "Okay, but how do I check out his computer if it is there? Where do I look for proof of his writing or having business with Biltmore? Wait, how do you even buy an airline ticket? Like you said, I'm a nun, and not of the flying variety. Maybe I should stay here, maybe we could ask someone else to go."

"Do you want to find and talk to Mr. Biltmore instead? Can you get him to confide in you about his relationship with the victim, find out why he left town, why he had a page with the name of Cheston's film written on it at his property, and who he's been talking to in Madrid about the murder?"

Eve blew out a breath. She wanted to go to California. Even though flying to a city alone was something she had never done before, she didn't feel afraid. In fact, the idea sounded appealing. She knew she was scheduled to have a conference call with her superiors in Pecos and that she needed to spend some time preparing for the conversation, but she wanted to find out more about this case. She wanted to dig up more information about the murder of Megan's boyfriend. Besides, she knew that the Captain shouldn't be negotiating airports and taxis—he had no business trying to travel in his condition. And she knew that if she didn't make the trip, he would find and talk to Mr. Biltmore and book a flight to L.A. too. Besides, the fact that he no longer had an associate in Los Angeles sounded like her doing. She sat up in her seat and nodded. She was going to Los Angeles.

"Will you promise me you will take your antibiotics, monitor your blood sugar, and rest once every couple of hours?"

"Yes ma'am, Sister."

She paused.

"How will you get to Biltmore if he's even home from his trip?" she wanted to know. He still was not able to drive.

"I'll check around, make sure he's home, and then I'll ask Daniel to take me. It'll look more official if I have an actual police officer with me," he answered.

"And Daniel agreed to this?"

"Well, not yet. But I don't think it will be a problem. It doesn't look like Hinds or anybody else in the department even has Biltmore on their radar. I think if I can get to him first, he'll give me all the information I want. Daniel shouldn't worry about having any conflict of interest."

"Except that he was warned not to talk to you about the case."

He shrugged. "We won't talk about the case. We'll talk about trips to India and property crime in Santa Fe County."

Eve folded her arms across her chest. She figured Daniel could make up his own mind about getting the Captain to Biltmore. She didn't need to worry about that.

"How did you even find out he was coming back to New Mexico?"

"I talked to his travel agent," he answered.

She shook her head. "I don't think I even want to know the details."

"No, probably not." He yawned.

"But you're sure he's coming back?" She started to get up. She could see he needed to rest.

"He booked his return flight for tomorrow afternoon. I'm

planning to make a visit to his place tomorrow evening, introduce myself, and find out what he knows."

Eve nodded. "So, this flight to Los Angeles, who do I call to reserve a ticket?"

Jackson leaned back and closed his eyes. "Not to worry. The ticket is in the top drawer of my desk at the office. I booked you on the two o'clock flight tomorrow afternoon."

"You did what?" She was surprised to hear this announcement.

"Two o'clock, Albuquerque to L.A. Take a sweater. It sometimes can get a little chilly on the planes." And he yawned once more. "Can you close the door on your way out? And the light, do turn off the light."

Evangeline waited a second and was about to say something about his presumptuous behavior, but she could see it would do no good. She shook her head, flipped off the overhead light, and pulled the door closed.

"I guess I'm going to California," she muttered to herself. "Wonder what the vice superior of the abbey will think of that." And she headed down the hall in the direction of her room. She would need to think about what to pack.

FORTY-NINE

———— ✦❋✦ ————

Eve wore her best pair of jeans and a blouse she'd found in her mother's old things. She wore her nicest boots and packed a small bag Dorisanne had left in her room. She took only a few items with her—her files and papers, a few toiletries, a toothbrush, and a flashlight, a T-shirt, a pair of the Captain's sweatpants, another pair of socks, and a lightweight jacket.

She arrived about an hour before her flight and struggled only a bit in the security line, forgetting to take off her belt, setting off the alarm with the rosary she kept in her front pocket, and then again with the prayer book she had forgotten in the back pocket of her pants. For the most part, though, she sailed through every check-in detail, boarding procedure, and taxi line. Nothing about the flight or navigating the airports had been all that challenging, and much to her surprise she even began to feel as if she had a knack for travel.

"Here's the address where I need to go," she said to the cabdriver after waiting in line and finally being motioned to the taxi at the end of the curb. She handed him the piece of paper that Megan had used to jot down where she lived, opened the door, and got in the backseat, her overnight bag at her feet.

She reached into the outside pouch of the small suitcase and found the key Megan had given her. She went over the plan again. She was to look around the house and see if she could find anything that would establish a connection or relationship of Cheston's that could shed light on who might have wanted him dead. The Captain had given her some ideas of what to look for—letters, computer files, phone records, but actually, there wasn't really any particular item she was trying to find. She was sent to L.A. to find answers to questions that had not even been asked.

She was also sent to see what had been taken from the house by the police. The Captain had been shown the search warrant request and return—the list of all items seized from the residence. Megan's lawyer had been given a copy, but Eve was supposed to make sure nothing else had been taken. Megan had given as detailed an account of her personal items in the house as she could remember, but that had been a hard assignment for the young woman to complete.

Eve recalled the questions the Captain had asked Megan on the phone the night before. "Did you have a calendar? Did you keep a diary? What kinds of files do you have on your desk? And Chaz?" He was taking copious notes that he gave Eve before she left. "What did he keep at the house? Is there another computer? Cell phones? Does he keep any records there?"

"First time in L.A.?"

Evangeline had stopped rifling through her papers and files and had practically pressed her nose to the window, peering at the sights as they drove out of the airport and in the direction of her destination. She smiled. "First time anywhere," she answered.

The cabdriver looked at her in his rearview mirror. "You here for business?"

Eve glanced back at him. He was dark-skinned, thin, and appeared young. She noticed his identification card on the dashboard of the car. She thought his name was African. She considered what had been asked. *Is this business?* she wondered. And when had she ever been asked such a question?

"I guess so, yes," she said.

He grinned. "Movie business?"

She shook her head. "Oh no, not that kind of business." And then the curiosity overcame her. "What makes you ask that?"

He lifted and dropped his shoulders as he merged onto the freeway, looking left and right. "The address," he replied, his accent thick. "Movie people's neighborhood."

She nodded. "Oh, right." And it dawned on her again just whose house she was visiting. She wondered if he would recognize the name of Megan Flint but decided it might not be prudent giving out her friend's information.

"Where are you from, Berihun?" she asked, calling out the name she could see printed on the card slid inside the plastic holder. She hoped she was pronouncing it correctly. She made a stab at the first name, knowing she wasn't going to attempt the last.

He sat up, watching her more closely in his mirror. "Ethiopia," he replied, his grin still wide. "I come to Los Angeles five years ago," he added.

"And was this a good move for you?" She quit watching the

sights outside her window and turned her attention to her driver. She realized she rarely had the chance to cross international lines and have a conversation with someone from another continent.

"Yes," he answered. "Very good. I come to make a place for my family. I make a home and send for my wife and children. I miss them very much, but I know they will soon join me."

Evangeline nodded. It was easy to see what being in America meant to him. "How did you choose California as your destination?"

"I pray for God to show me."

Evangeline glanced away. The city was coming into view. *So this is Los Angeles*, she thought, *the City of Angels*. She thought about his answer, and she wondered if divine intervention had in fact brought the young man from Africa to America, if that was what had brought him to Los Angeles. She wondered if it had been divine intervention that had taken her from the convent in Pecos back to her home in Madrid, from the kneeling bench to her father's bedside. She wondered if it had all been part of some divine plan that she was sitting in a cab on her way to a movie star's house. Was it divine intervention that was taking place in her life at that very moment?

Evangeline faced ahead and studied the man's reflection in the small mirror in the center of the windshield. She could see his sincerity, even his joy in the narrow view she had of his eyes, his smile when he raised his face. She thought of her own situation and wondered if she had the kind of faith the driver seemed to have. She thought about the previous night's conversation she'd had with the vice superior.

She had explained about the Captain's setback, the infection, the fact that he still was not able to drive. "How much longer do you need?" the vice superior had asked after agreeing to the request, and

Eve had not known how to respond. "Six weeks should be enough," she had answered, recalling the conversation she'd had earlier with the nurse. The Captain could drive in three. She had felt a sense of guilt, even though her superior said the six weeks was fine.

"What does *Berihun* mean?" she asked, shaking aside the thoughts of the previous night's phone conversation.

His grin widened. "'Let him guide us,'" he answered. "My parents were very religious people, so I was put in God's hands even before I was born."

"Then it looks like they gave you the perfect name."

"I always feel my face was turned in the right way." He paused, showing a lack of confidence in his English translation. "Do you know what I mean?" he asked. "Is that the correct way to say?"

She nodded. "I understand what you mean exactly." She closed her eyes and leaned her head against the back of the seat.

She recalled having felt that way once herself. She had left for the convent when she was probably the same age as her driver, Berihun, and she had felt exactly the way he had described his life, his decision—that her face was turned in the right way. *Now, here I am, not sure which way my face is turned. Flying on an airplane, doing the work of a detective, solving a mystery. Has my face turned and I was not paying attention?*

"And your name," he responded. "Is there meaning to your name?"

She sat up and watched as he turned into a neighborhood where all the houses were secured behind tall iron gates. It was a neighborhood like she had never seen before.

"Evangeline," she answered. "My name is Evangeline." She read the house number on the gate as they approached.

The car slowed as they pulled into the driveway and stopped.

She smiled. "It's supposed to mean 'bearer of good news,'" she added.

"And your parents," Berihun said as he punched the Stop button on the meter and totaled up the fare. "Did they give you the perfect name as well?"

Eve reached into her purse and pulled out the slip of paper with Megan's pass code. She handed it to the driver. He inched forward, punched in the code, and handed the paper back to Eve. The gate opened and he headed to the front of the house.

"I'm not sure, Berihun," she replied. "I'm not sure all my news is good."

The driver grinned and stopped the taxi. He put the car in park and exited the driver's side. He walked around and opened the door for Eve.

"You must not worry that you bear only good news," he said, extending his hand. "You must only be sure to bear what is true."

Evangeline took the man's hand and got out of the car, grabbing her bag. She reached into her wallet that she had already taken out and handed the driver the fare she had seen displayed on the meter plus a few extra dollars for a tip. As she did so, she could not help but recall the end of her conversation with the director of the abbey, the question she was asked after receiving his permission for the extension.

"Are you eager to come back?" he had asked. And a long pause followed. "Of course," she had answered and swiftly hung up the phone, the reply hanging in the air like a thick, full cloud.

She smiled at her driver. "Unfortunately, Berihun, I don't always bear that kind of news either."

FIFTY

✦❋✦

"There was nothing much there," she reported to the Captain as she stood in the phone booth at the Albuquerque airport. She had just gotten off the plane and thought she would make a quick call to let him know she had arrived safely back in New Mexico. That ended up taking awhile, though, since pay phones were not nearly as plentiful in public areas as she had once remembered.

"Yeah, you told me that last night," came the response. "Just a calendar."

"And the other things," she added. She had called with the same report the previous evening after searching Megan's house for three hours. She had checked for the items taken that were listed in the search warrant return—all indeed missing—and she had looked in cabinets and drawers and closets and searched shelves. She hadn't located much of anything that would have a bearing on Megan's defense or in presenting another suspect.

According to the young woman, the house was hers but had

been paid for by the victim. Everything inside appeared to be that of one resident, a female, Evangeline thought, but there was clearly evidence that a man stayed there regularly. The furniture, the fixtures, the decorations, all bore a certain feminine quality, and everything seemed to be in line with what she had been told by Megan. It was a beautiful residence, the nicest Eve had ever been in, and, primarily, the house bore a woman's touch.

There was one room, Eve had noted, a room in the back that had obviously been turned into an office. It was the only area where the furniture was masculine, the accessories unmatched, and everything in a bit of disarray. When she had spoken to Megan after discovering the room, calling her in Santa Fe, she had been told that it was Cheston's office and that she rarely went back there. Evangeline was given permission to take a look around and so she searched very thoroughly.

She found nothing she would deem remarkable inside the desk drawers. The file cabinets, the ones that had not been emptied, were filled with scripts and notes from other projects, and the bookcase lining a wall had long, narrow shelves loaded with film books, novels, and other pieces of literature, but nothing too revealing.

A calendar that hung on the wall next to the desk caught Eve's eye. It had the name of a bank stamped on the back. It was one of the free ones you get when you open an account or take out a loan. This one featured monthly pictures from a wildlife conservation group. There were a few scribbles written on various dates, numbers mostly, a few letters with them—notes made throughout the months of February and March that at first glance were indecipherable. Even though Eve didn't know what the letters and numbers meant, she thought the calendar could possibly hold some value, so she had taken it off the wall. Other than the calendar, all that Eve collected to take back with her was a file containing a few pages of information about possible filming locations in Madrid, Cerrillos, and Santa Fe County, and a small box of CDs and DVDs.

Megan had made a list of some items she wanted, so Eve packed a suitcase she found in the main bedroom's closet with the desired clothes and shoes and then added the few things from Cheston's office. She did find a gun in a shoebox on the top shelf while packing the bag, but she knew she would not be able to carry that back on the plane so she simply made a note for herself to tell the Captain and to ask Megan whose it was and what it was doing in her bedroom.

"There were no bank statements?" the Captain asked.

"Wait, how did you get to your office?" She had tried to reach him at home when she first called and there was no answer. On a whim, she had decided to call his office, and he had surprised her by picking up the phone. "Tell me you didn't drive."

"Marcie came by," he answered.

Eve knew he meant Marcie Lunez, the owner of the Mineshaft. *How thoughtful of her to check on him*, Eve thought.

"Bank statements," he said again, trying to get her back to the subject at hand.

"No bank statements, no files about money or wire transfers, no credit card information, no bills, nothing like that anywhere," she replied.

The absence of such day-to-day paperwork surprised her at first, but then again, she knew the police had confiscated anything related to the victim's business records. She still wasn't sure she understood that as being necessary to the prosecution, but the Captain had explained that sometimes what was necessary to the district attorney included anything that might be helpful to the defense.

She heard a long breath pouring across the phone lines.

"I did find some files about his latest movie project," she said, hoping that might be something interesting he would like to hear.

"Any budget information?"

She sighed. "No, just location stuff."

"How about an address book or phone log?"

She hated having nothing substantial to report. Surely paying for an unnecessary trip to L.A. would not help the Captain's financial situation. She felt guilty.

"Oh, just never mind," he said, reading into the silence. "Why are you calling me from the airport anyway? Why aren't you just heading home?"

"I wanted to let you know that I was back in New Mexico," she replied, thinking she should have known her polite act would not be appreciated. "If you don't need me right away, I'll go to Santa Fe and drop off the things Megan wanted. I won't be back to Madrid until a little later this afternoon."

"Oh," he growled. "Okay, then, I'll see you when you get home."

Evangeline wanted to know about his work and was just about to ask how his conversation had gone with Mr. Biltmore when she suddenly noticed John Ewing walking past her toward the security area. She wondered if he was taking a trip, but could see that he was not carrying any bag or holding a ticket in his hand.

"Did you talk to Ross Biltmore?" she asked.

"His plane was delayed," came the answer. "Comes in today. He got stuck in Chicago, snowstorm," he added. "Daniel is supposed to come by for supper. We hope we can get to him then."

"You talk to the travel agent again?"

"You know, I kind of like her. She's very knowledgeable about international travel. And she has been very helpful in getting flight information."

"You planning on making a trip?" she asked. She glanced around but couldn't see the old rancher any longer.

"You never know what the future might bring," he said.

It was then that she noticed a flight had arrived and the airport was filling up with passengers coming off a plane. She thought she saw Ewing again. He was standing in the waiting area.

"What time today?" she asked.

"What time today what?" It seemed he was not following her.

"What time today was Biltmore coming in?"

But before he could answer, she asked another question. "Is Biltmore kind of short, keeps a beard, long hair, wears glasses?"

"What?"

"Biltmore," she repeated his name. "Do you know what he looks like?"

"Mid-fifties, I guess. From a photograph I saw he has salt-and-pepper hair, keeps it in a ponytail. He did have a beard, and yes, he wears wire rims. And according to your friend Madeline, he's usually in jeans and a brown leather jacket, the kind hippies are always wearing."

"With fringe," Eve noted.

"What?"

"Fringe."

"Yeah, I guess that's right."

There was a pause.

"Why are you asking about him anyway?"

"Because he's here," she said, watching the very intimate greeting between the Cerrillos rancher and the man the Captain had just described.

"What?"

"Ross Biltmore just flew in. You'll never guess who is welcoming him home."

And she lowered her head and turned her back to the crowd so that the two men would not notice her as they passed.

FIFTY-ONE

———— ⁘ ————

"Sister Evangeline, how was your trip to Los Angeles?" Ron Polland answered the door to the house where Megan was staying.

"How did you know I was in L.A.?" she asked.

"Megan tells me everything that's going on with her lawyer and her detective." He paused. "Or should I say detective*s*?" he asked, emphasizing the plural. He stepped aside so that she could enter.

"Is Megan here?" She didn't really like being around Polland.

"Of course she's here, Miss Divine, she's under house arrest." He turned and walked into the kitchen. "I'm having a drink. Can I fix you something?"

Eve stood at the door, deciding what to do. She certainly wasn't interested in having a drink with the producer, but she put down Megan's bag and followed him. "It's not Divine, it's pronounced *Diveen*." She was pretty sure she had told him this once before.

"Oh, right," he replied. "Megan's getting a massage," he said, finally getting around to answering the question. "She'll be available in an hour." He got a few ice cubes from the freezer and put them in a glass. "I'm having scotch and soda," he announced. He turned to face Eve. He seemed to be waiting for a response.

"No, nothing," she said. "I just had a Coke on the airplane."

"Did you fly out of Santa Fe?" He seemed surprised.

She shook her head. "Albuquerque."

"Then that had to be over an hour ago."

She nodded.

He took a sip. "You can have something else to drink, if you like." He studied her. "Are you only allowed one drink a day?"

The question confused her. "No."

He shook his head. "Never mind." He walked past her toward the large living room where she had visited with Megan previously. "Let's go in here," he said.

Eve paused. She hadn't really intended to stay, and she certainly hadn't planned on having a conversation with Ron Polland.

"Sister," he called out.

And she headed in his direction.

He was already seated on the sofa. She sat in the chair opposite him.

"How did you find things at Megan's house?" he asked.

She shrugged. "I guess everything is fine."

"Yes, I sent my assistant over there a few days ago. She said that the police had confiscated a few things, but they hadn't made a mess." He brought the glass to his lips for another drink. "You never know," he added.

Eve chose not to comment.

"Did you find anything helpful to the case?"

She waited, thinking about the question and the one who was asking. She wasn't sure she wanted to give Polland any more information than he seemed to have already. She knew that Megan was grateful to him for posting her bail and getting her the house to stay in, but Evangeline wasn't so certain about the man's motives. "I thought Cheston's calendar was interesting." She decided to put it out there just to see a response.

"His personal calendar?"

She shook her head. "A calendar pinned to the wall beside his desk. It had a few notes on it for the months he was in New Mexico."

He perked up. "Like reservation information for a car or the rental house?"

"No, I wouldn't say that."

"Confirmation numbers?"

She hadn't thought of that.

"Passwords?"

That was exactly what it could be, she thought. But she also thought she didn't need to tell him. She shook her head. "I don't think it's anything," she replied.

He took another swallow, nodding his head.

"I didn't see a car in the driveway," she noted. "Did you drive here?"

He stretched out his legs in front of him. "No, I use a car service when I'm in town."

She nodded. "Los Angeles seems like a hard place to get around, so much traffic. Do you drive yourself when you're there?"

"I have a driver," he answered.

She was thinking.

"But I like to drive," he answered without a prompt.

"Yeah? Me too." She offered her best fake smile.

"Get to drive a lot at the convent, do you?" he asked.

She shrugged. "Well, we don't have a popemobile, but yes, I get around."

He grinned.

"So, what kind of vehicle do you have?"

She was still interested in the report of the dark SUV with California plates seen on the dirt road the day Cheston disappeared, the one near the librarian's house. Maybe she'd get lucky and that's exactly the kind of vehicle he drove. She waited for the answer.

FIFTY-TWO

Polland eyed her as if he knew the question was more than just a chance to make small talk. "Porsche," he replied. "I like sports cars."

She nodded. It was not the answer she was hoping for.

"You don't trust me, do you, Sister?" He finished his drink, setting the glass on the table beside the sofa.

"I'm not sure I know what you mean."

"I mean, you think my relationship with Megan isn't just about me looking out for her. You think I have some hidden motive for all that I'm doing." He leaned forward, resting his elbows on his knees.

"Well, do you?" She locked eyes with him.

He grinned and sat back, throwing one leg over the other and dropping his hands in his lap. He seemed relaxed, comfortable. "I warned Megan not to get involved with Chaz. I've known the man a long time. He was no good for her."

"Then why did you send her here to try and find him when he disappeared?"

"Because I thought she would have a better shot of locating him than I would."

"Because the two of you were fighting? Because he owed you money or you didn't think he was going to get the script finished on time?"

Polland gave a chuckle. "You think I killed Charles Cheston? You think I paid Megan's bail and got her this house, medications, a massage therapist, because I want to see her fry for a murder she didn't commit?"

Eve didn't answer.

"Tell me, Sister, did they teach you this demeanor of suspicion, or is this the vice you're trying to overcome at the convent?"

"I didn't become a nun to overcome a vice," she said.

"No?"

"No," she answered.

He shrugged. "When I was in seminary, I met a lot of young men joining the priesthood in an attempt to run away from something."

She didn't respond. "I suppose there are people who take vows to remove themselves from the things of this world."

He smiled.

"That was not my reason," she added.

"Okay," he said. "Maybe not, but still, you strike me as having a bit more going on than just a desire to help the poor."

"Maybe there's a desire to help those being exploited as well as the poor," she responded.

"And that's what you think about Megan?"

"You do seem to have quite a hold on her," Eve noted.

"I'll answer your questions about Cheston, Sister." He cleared his throat. "Charles was a talented writer and director. I needed him to finish this project. We had a lot of money riding on this film of his, and I had given him way too much room to do things his way. But time and money had run out, and I'm pretty sure Cheston was stealing from me." He said this with an angry tone.

Evangeline was about to ask a follow-up question about why he thought such a thing and whether or not there was proof of the theft, but he kept going.

"This was going to be my last title with him. He was too much trouble, cost me too much money. And let me tell you one thing: He may have cleaned up for a couple of weeks, but I know, excuse me, I knew Charles Cheston better than anyone." He sat up and pointed his finger for emphasis. "If he hadn't yet, he was going to fall off that wagon, and I told him that I was done rescuing him. This was his last chance."

He sat back, sliding his hands through his hair.

"Why did Megan stay with him if he was such trouble?" Eve wanted to know his take on the relationship between the young woman and the victim.

Polland laughed and shook his head. "Well, you're right about her. Megan is naive. She's a gullible, credulous child. She believed him when he said he was divorcing his wife. She believed him when he said he stopped using drugs. She believed him when he said he loved her. And none of that was true. If she committed this murder, believe me, I'm sure he deserved it. As far as I'm concerned, she shouldn't have to suffer one minute if she did kill him. He was a junkie and a thief. And his Hollywood merry-go-round was about to come to an end one way or the other, and she shouldn't have to lose her career just because he was losing his."

He stopped.

Evangeline had turned away and was no longer watching him.

"What? Am I not interesting enough to hold your attention?" He glanced over to where she appeared to be looking.

"Megan," she called out.

But it was too late. The young woman had heard everything.

FIFTY-THREE

―――――⟨✳⟩――――――

"So, let me get this straight . . ." The Captain was sitting in the wheelchair with Trooper on his lap. He had explained that his arms were tired from using the crutches. "You saw John Ewing meet Ross Biltmore at the airport."

Eve nodded. She was slicing a roast she had bought in Madrid after returning from Santa Fe. It was dinnertime, and she had prepared a meal for them both.

"And it was friendly?"

She looked up at him as she placed the slices of meat on the two plates. "I'd say it was more than friendly." She spooned some green beans next.

"I don't understand," he replied.

"It appeared as if Mr. Ewing and Mr. Biltmore were extremely happy to see each other."

He still appeared confused.

"They looked like a couple," she said.

"Ewing is a homosexual?" He was shaking his head. "How could I miss that?"

She pulled two slices of bread from a bag on the counter, placed them on the plates, and walked over to the table to set them down before heading back to the kitchen. "It's not usually anything people advertise, especially out here." She poured two glasses of milk.

"What does that mean?" He wheeled himself over to his place at the table and nudged Trooper. The dog scooted off his lap.

She set down the drinks. "It means there are a lot of gay people in our lives—they just don't go around making it public." She took her seat.

"Yeah, but that's something I usually get right away. I've known John Ewing for forty years." He put his napkin in his lap.

Evangeline bowed her head and prayed. She crossed herself and took a sip from her milk. "Does it matter?" She reached for her fork.

He shrugged. "Nah, not to me." He took a bite of his supper. "What do I care about somebody's personal business? Does it matter to you?"

Eve hesitated. She hadn't really thought about whether or not it mattered to her. There had been more than a few conversations at the convent about homosexuality. She had been given lots of rules and read doctrines on the subject. She had even heard the confessions of a few nuns who were gay. Ultimately, she had decided it wasn't really her place to judge anyone else, but she hadn't expected that she would land at the same place as her father. She just shook her head and kept watching him.

"What?" he asked, chewing.

"Nothing," she replied. "You just surprise me is all."

"You think I'd cause trouble for Ewing knowing this about him?"

She shrugged.

"Then you don't know me very well," he added.

She nodded, even though she had a hard time believing that statement. She was pretty certain she knew the Captain better than anyone else.

"Okay, so what if Biltmore and Ewing are a couple?" He wiped his mouth. "Why would they want Cheston dead?"

"Well, maybe it's a love triangle," Eve guessed.

"I suspect Megan would have a hard time believing Cheston was gay," he suggested.

Evangeline remembered how Megan looked when she had heard all the things that Polland had to say about Cheston, about her. She wondered if the two of them had made up, if Polland had gotten her to unlock the bedroom door and talk to him, something that hadn't happened before Eve had left the house.

"Maybe the couple didn't murder Cheston. Maybe Biltmore and Cheston had a fight about the book or the story that we're guessing Biltmore was writing for him, he killed Cheston, and Ewing is just helping him cover it up." She was trying to figure out another motive for Biltmore to murder his old college roommate.

"Could be," the Captain responded. "If I recall, John did act very nervous when we visited him at the Silver Cross. I wouldn't be surprised at all that he helped Biltmore get out of town and has been in touch with him ever since."

"And why would he come back now?" Eve wondered out loud.

"Well, he knew Daniel and I were checking out his property. Maybe he felt like he needed to be here to make sure nothing else is discovered." He took another bite of roast.

Eve nodded. That made sense to her.

"Or maybe he's come back to confess."

Eve smiled. "Well, that would make things a lot easier for us, wouldn't it?" She took another bite of her meal.

"Now, tell me what happened with Polland."

Eve finished her bite. "He drives a Porsche," she replied.

"Okay," the Captain replied. "Why is that important?"

"It wasn't a Porsche that Miss Buttercup saw at the intersection."

"He could have rented a black SUV and driven here," he added.

Eve hadn't thought of that. "Right."

"But he admitted that he thought Cheston was stealing from him?" The Captain had heard some of what had happened in Santa Fe when Eve first got home.

"That's what he seems to think. He didn't give me any details. He just said he was sure Cheston was headed toward using drugs again if he wasn't already and that this was Polland's last project with him." She took a swallow of her milk. "Maybe he had told Cheston that and they got in a fight?"

The Captain nodded. "Could be," he said. "But I think if he had come here to New Mexico the night Cheston disappeared, Megan would have seen him. He had no reason to hide if he came to confront Cheston."

"Maybe she's covering for him?"

"If she was, and she was as upset as you say she was after hearing Polland say all those things, she likely won't be covering for him much longer. All that will take is a phone call." He finished his supper and wiped his mouth. He folded the napkin and placed it beside the plate. "So, tell me about Los Angeles."

She was still eating. "I liked it," she said. "It's big and spread out and I'd never want to live there, but it's a nice city."

He was staring at her. "I'm talking about what you found at Megan's house."

"Oh." She dabbed at the corners of her mouth. "It's like I said, I didn't find much. Everything on the list you gave me was definitely missing. There was no computer of any kind, no cell phones, no related files other than the one I brought back that contained information on filming locations."

"You said you took a calendar?"

She nodded. "It was hanging on the wall beside his desk. It just had a few notes on it, and I thought they might mean something. It had a bank's name stamped on it." She suddenly thought of her conversation with Polland. "It could be passwords to an account or something." She wrinkled up her nose. "How would we check that out?"

"We could find out where he had bank accounts, see if the codes work. What bank did that calendar come from?"

"I'm not sure. I'll have to take another look at it."

"We can google the bank, give the number and the codes you found, and see if they are valid account numbers or passwords."

This impressed her. "Oh, and there was a gun," she remembered.

"A gun?"

"It was in Megan's closet, in a shoebox."

The Captain seemed to be thinking about this news. "Well,

since a gun was not the murder weapon, I guess it doesn't matter if Megan had a gun or not." He shook his head. "What else?"

"Nothing much," she replied. "The CDs, DVDs, and the file. Nothing that appears to support the theory that Cheston was killed by Megan or by anybody else. Inside it was just a regular house."

"But you wouldn't want to live there?" he teased.

Evangeline was just about to respond when a knock on the door interrupted her. She stood up.

"It's probably Daniel," the Captain noted. "We're going over to Biltmore's again later."

Evangeline opened the front door and stood there for a moment without saying a word.

"Well, don't just stand there, Eve, let him in."

"It's not a him," came the response from the other side of the door.

Trooper began to bark.

"Hello, Eve, Captain."

And Evangeline opened the screen door and stepped aside so that her sister could make her way into the house.

FIFTY-FOUR

Eve left so that Dorisanne could have a little time alone with the Captain. Neither one of them asked for it. She just thought that the two of them should have their own private conversation. She had fixed a plate for Dorisanne, cleaned up the dishes, and given the Captain his insulin. She told them that she was going to visit Madeline and chose not to mention that on her way she would stop and introduce herself to Mr. Biltmore. She knew the Captain would disallow such a meeting, even if she promised that she would not confront him or ask any questions about his relationship with the victim, but she was feeling confident after making a trip to California and after having what she thought was a productive conversation with Ron Polland.

She headed down the highway and made the turn onto the dirt road. She glanced over to her right and saw the lights on at Miss Buttercup's house. She wondered if the librarian was watching and taking notes of whose truck was heading west on the dirt road.

She kept going and thought about Dorisanne and the conversation that was being held in the dining room of her parents' house. She hoped her sister wouldn't get mad and leave too quickly and that the Captain would be on his best behavior.

Once she started thinking about what might be happening between the two remaining members of her family, she slowed down and considered turning around and going back, taking on the role of mediator between the two, a role she used to step into very easily when she was younger. But instead, she sped up. Dorisanne was old enough to manage her own discussions, and the Captain needed to learn how to deal with his own messes. If she had learned anything from living in community, Eve was clear on the lesson that not every drama needed to be her drama.

She lightly touched the brakes as she passed over each cattle guard and could see the lights on at the Biltmore cabin a couple of miles before she got to the gated driveway. She thought about what she would say when Biltmore opened the door.

"I'll just say I was at Madeline's and hadn't met him, saw that he was home, and thought I'd drop by," she said out loud. *It's mostly true*, she thought, and then recalled the L.A. taxi driver's comments and how short she was falling of bearing only the truth. "Or, I could say that I'm working on a murder case and have no idea what I'm doing."

She stopped when she made it over the last cattle guard and saw that the gate to the property was closed. She thought about her options. She knew the Captain would be very angry about her decision, but she parked the truck on the side of the road as she had done once before—only this time right in front of the driveway—turned off the engine, got out, and jumped the gate. She also remembered a promise she had made about not doing this kind of thing again. It had been in a prayer. She stopped and made the sign of the cross. She would be in confession by the end of the week, and she knew what she'd be confessing. *I'll be quick*, she told herself, thinking a speedy trespass was somehow less offensive.

Eve was happy that she was wearing sneakers and had an easier time making the hike from the end of the driveway to the cabin. She walked the distance in a much shorter amount of time than she had when wearing the clogs. She headed up the path and noticed the truck by the porch. She had seen it before at the Silver Cross. Ewing was still with Mr. Biltmore.

She stopped at the back of the vehicle, trying to get an idea of where the two men might be and where she would have the best chance of observing them without being noticed. She glanced over at the house and peered in through the open windows. She immediately saw the rancher sitting on a barstool in the kitchen. She thought she could see Mr. Biltmore moving around near the stove and sink. She guessed that he was preparing a meal. She could hear the sound of two men talking. She moved a little closer and crouched down on the porch between the front door and the window.

"If he picked up the script, then where's the money?" It was Mr. Ewing's voice.

"I don't know," came the reply. "I just know that the safe was empty and that's where he was supposed to leave it."

"Maybe somebody else was here," Ewing said.

"It seems unlikely," Biltmore responded. "I mean, I talked to him the night before he was coming over. He was the only one who knew where I had hidden the pages."

"Do you have any whiskey?"

"Top drawer of the desk."

She heard the stool move and footsteps coming toward her. A drawer opened and closed, and she remembered having seen that Biltmore's desk was situated near the window, not far from where she was hiding.

"How much was supposed to be there?"

She guessed Ewing was standing right next to her.

"Twenty-five thousand," Biltmore replied.

He was so close to her she could hear the man breathing. Then he turned and headed back to the kitchen.

There were the sounds of ice cubes dropping into a glass and the stool sliding back out. "And none of it was there?"

"Nothing. I told you. He took the pages and left me nothing."

Eve could hear sounds from the stove, popping, frying noises. She scooted up a bit because she was having a difficult time making out the voices. When she did, she kicked her foot out and banged into the rocking chair that she was crouched behind. It slipped forward.

"What was that?"

Eve quickly jumped up and hurried away from the porch, finding a hiding place behind Mr. Ewing's truck.

The front door opened. A light came on. She was squatting behind the back tire. She held her breath.

"Probably just the wind."

There was a long pause when she could hear nothing. And the

door closed. Eve exhaled. She waited, unable to hear anything else, and then she stood, carefully, slowly, keeping her body pressed to the truck. She was at the rear of the bed on the passenger's side.

She hesitated a bit longer and then lifted her head to look across the truck toward the porch. The coast appeared to be clear, and she was about to head back at full speed to the gate and into her vehicle, having a close enough call, when something caught her eye in the bed of the truck. It was a slip of paper sticking out of the equipment box bolted behind the cab. She pushed on the lid and it opened, and the paper, which she didn't catch a good look at, sailed past her.

She was closing the lid as quietly as she could when she noticed something odd. Inside the equipment box was something shaped almost like a gun, but with the porch light on, she could just make out that it was not a firearm. It was something else, she thought, and then she remembered the vaccine injector used at the clinic in Cerrillos when she was a child. It had been explained to her that the stainless-steel medical device used a high-pressure jet of compressed air to administer medicine rather than a hypodermic needle. She recalled that the shot had stung a bit. As far as she knew, they didn't use them any longer because of the hepatitis scare and the possibility of contamination.

She was reaching in to pick up the contraption and get a closer look when she felt a hand suddenly reach across her face and fingers tightly clamp her mouth.

She heard a whisper, "Don't make a sound," and she was immediately pulled back down behind the truck.

FIFTY-FIVE

"If your daddy knew what you were doing, he'd have your hide. And it doesn't matter one bit that you're too old to get whipped or that you're a nun!" Daniel spoke in a harsh whisper. He held on to the collar of Evangeline's shirt and escorted her away from the truck and down the path back to the end of the driveway.

She didn't say a word until he had hoisted her over the gate and they were standing at her vehicle. "Geez, Daniel, you almost gave me a heart attack!" She rubbed her neck. "What are you doing out here?" she asked.

"What am I doing out here?" he repeated. "That's my question. What are you doing trespassing again? Didn't you learn your lesson the first time?"

Daniel was dressed in a suit, the same attire she was used to seeing him in when he was at work. He was sweating a bit and he had leaned over, dropping his hands on his knees. She could see the firearm on his belt, his badge, and a cell phone.

"Why are you breathing so heavy?"

"Because as soon as I saw the truck and knew it was you making an unlawful entry again and knowing that Biltmore was home and could be very unhappy about a trespasser on his property, I parked and ran up the driveway to see what kind of mess you were making for yourself. That's a long haul up to the cabin."

He was right, Eve thought. It was a lot harder going up the path to the house than coming down. And she had never run it. She glanced around for Daniel's car. "Where did you park?"

"About half a mile up the road," he answered.

His fatigue was making a lot more sense. He had covered quite a distance before getting to her.

"If you hadn't yet been discovered, I didn't want to give anybody a reason to call Biltmore and tell him he had two vehicles parked at the end of his driveway, one a police car. Your truck is suspicious enough." He was still trying to catch his breath.

Eve nodded. "Were you going to go visit Biltmore?"

"That was the plan," he said, pulling a handkerchief out of his back pocket and wiping his face. "I stopped by your dad's place and saw that he was busy with Dorisanne, so I told him I'd just come by and make an initial contact, see what I might find out. Little did I know Sister Ethan Hunt was out here snooping around."

"Who's Ethan Hunt?"

He shook his head. "Tom Cruise in the *Mission Impossible* series."

"What happened to Peter Graves?" She used to watch the television series reruns and loved the main character from the drama filmed in the seventies.

"Died in 2010. He was eighty-three," Daniel replied. "The first new *Mission Impossible* with Tom Cruise came out in 1996." He studied her. "Are you telling me you haven't seen a movie since 1996? That's a lot longer than just six years. That's like—" He started counting.

"I know what it's like," she interrupted. "I just didn't see this movie. I've seen a movie since then."

He put the handkerchief back and rested his hands on his hips. "You never answered my question. What are you doing out here?"

She made a couple of shoulder rolls, a neck stretch, anything to avoid direct eye contact. "I saw Mr. Biltmore at the airport. I just thought I'd stop by."

"Did you speak to Mr. Biltmore?"

"Uh, no."

"Did you call him up and ask him if you could stop by?"

She shook her head.

"So, you knew this man was home, and you jumped his gate to trespass and spy on him?"

She shrugged. "You don't have to make it sound so much like a crime."

"Evangeline, it is a crime."

She played with her hair, smoothing it down on both sides, trying to pass off her best "I'm so innocent" look. She could see it wasn't working.

"Go on home," he said. "Go be with your sister and your dad."

"How's that going, anyway?" she asked. She thought she might prefer to wait a little longer.

"Seemed fine. I didn't see any evidence of plates being thrown, and as far as I know, there haven't been any complaints lodged by the neighbors regarding domestic violence. Besides, that's what I expected from you two, not Dorisanne."

Eve rolled her eyes. "Right, because she's the quiet one."

He walked over and opened the driver's-side door of the truck. Eve got the message and met him there.

"Aren't you going to ask me if I saw or heard anything interesting?"

He shook his head. "It wouldn't be prudent for a police officer to receive information that was obtained illegally."

She hadn't thought of that. She got in the truck and he shut the door. She started the engine and rolled down the window. He was still standing beside her.

"Hypothetically, why would somebody have a jet injector?" she asked.

"A what?"

"A jet injector, you know the kind they used to give vaccines to us in the seventies and eighties, the kind I think they still use in other countries." She thought she had remembered seeing pictures of Catholic mission work in third-world areas, some of which had to do with health care and vaccines being given to children.

He shook his head. "Could be somebody has to give shots to horses, use it for a tranquilizer for mountain lions or bears. I'm not sure." He studied her. "You see something like that up there?"

"I thought you didn't want to hear anything that might have been obtained without a proper search warrant." She faced ahead.

"Listen to you. When did you start talking like this?"

"What?"

"How do you know anything about proper search warrants?"

She was about to answer when they both turned to see lights coming from the cabin in their direction. Somebody was heading toward them, and he or she seemed to be driving very fast.

FIFTY-SIX

———— ⁂ ————

"Watch out!" Evangeline shouted, and Daniel quickly jumped away from the vehicle that they were both sure was going to be T-boned by the truck careening toward the end of the driveway and just about to plow through the gate.

Evangeline faced forward and braced herself, still holding on to the steering wheel. She squeezed her eyes tightly and held her breath. There was a moment of utter shock when she realized that the truck had come to a screeching halt just on the other side of the gate.

There was gravel flying and swirls of dust everywhere. Then a door opened, and a bright light was shining in Evangeline's eyes. She held up her hand, blocking the glare.

"Who's out here?"

Eve tried to gather herself, to steady her pulse and regain her breath. She glanced out the window of the driver's side. Daniel was nowhere to be seen. It dawned on her that he might have been injured when he jumped aside. She ignored the question she had been asked and opened the truck door, calling out his name.

"Daniel! Daniel!"

It was pitch-black except where the truck lights on the other side of the gate were shining and the lone beam coming from a flashlight that had been the glare in Eve's eyes. There was a sound of someone moving, and Eve hurried to the ditch on the other side of the road where she thought she had heard the noise.

Daniel was getting up from the ground. She could see him now in the lights. He was brushing off his clothes. "I'm right here," he finally answered.

Eve reached out her hand and he took it. She pulled and Daniel climbed out of the ditch and moved closer, bumping into her.

"Are you all right?" she asked.

"I'm fine," he answered, dropping her hand and trying to pick off the spiny barbs from the sticker bush he had landed in.

"Who's out there?" the voice from the other side of the gate called out again.

Daniel walked in the direction of the man. "Detective Daniel Hively." He moved around the truck.

She stayed put and could hear the gate being unlocked and opened. She could see Daniel handing over his identification.

"What's going on?"

And Eve recognized the voice as John Ewing's. She eased across the road and around the truck.

"Sister Evangeline?" He had the flashlight on her.

"Hello, Mr. Ewing," she replied. "What are you doing out here?"

He didn't respond. "I'm visiting . . ." He paused. "Well,

what about you? Did something happen out here? Why are the police here?"

"Oh, I, uh . . ."

"I used to be her father's partner," Daniel said, coming to her rescue. "She was driving me out to my car. You know, dead battery. I couldn't get a cell signal, so I walked to 14, made a call to the Divines, and waited until Evangeline met me there at the intersection."

Eve turned to him. It amazed her that he had come up with such a good story so quickly. It made perfect sense and likely would not be challenged. She was impressed.

Ewing glanced around. "Where's the car?"

Eve quickly turned to Daniel. She hadn't thought of that. Maybe Daniel's story wasn't as good as she thought.

"That's the thing," he said, his voice calm, steady. "We stopped here because I couldn't quite remember how far up the road it was."

She nodded, looked back at the rancher, and smiled.

"You out here on police business?" He had put the flash-light down.

Eve waited.

"Murder victim's car was found up the road a ways. I was checking out the area again, making sure we didn't miss anything."

"Can't see much in the dark," Ewing noted.

"It wasn't dark when I was up there."

Daniel was not about to be outwitted, Eve thought.

"When that sun sets, though . . . Well, let's just say I wasn't quite prepared for this." He had his hands on his hips again.

Eve could see that his suit jacket had gotten torn in his jump into the ditch. He was also covered in dust.

Ewing handed him back his identification.

"You seemed like you were in a real hurry," Daniel said. "I was sure you were coming through that gate and into the side of Captain Divine's truck." He paused, putting the identification back in his pocket. "Everything okay with you?"

Ewing nodded, reached up, and scratched his chin. "Got a call from my stable man. One of the horses is foaling, having some trouble, he said. So I was in a bit of a hurry to get over there. I thought I had left the gate open when I drove in." He turned and looked at his truck. "Guess I'm glad I just replaced the brakes."

Daniel nodded. "We'll get out of your way, then," he said, gesturing to Eve.

She took that to mean he wanted her to move the truck, and she walked over to the driver's side.

"I think my car is just up the road there," he added.

Ewing looked toward the west, thinking the detective meant that direction. "All right," he said. "I hope you get to it okay." He turned to walk to his truck and turned back. "You need help with a jump?"

"With what?" Daniel asked.

"A jump," Ewing repeated. "You said your battery died. You need cables?"

Eve reached into the back of the Captain's truck. She held up a set of jumper cables. "We're all set," she answered for him.

Daniel turned, giving her a surprised look.

"Okay then," Ewing said. "Evangeline, tell your daddy hello. And nice to meet you, Detective."

"Yes, nice to meet you." He paused.

"Ewing," Eve whispered. "John Ewing."

"Mr. Ewing," he finished up his farewell. He opened the passenger's-side door and waved.

Eve got into the driver's side, turned on the engine, waited for Daniel to get in the car, and moved forward enough so that the rancher could ease past her onto the dirt road. "Well, that was a close one!"

Daniel just looked at her and shook his head. "Just drive me to my car," he said, sounding more than a little frustrated.

FIFTY-SEVEN

"And he almost hit you?" Dorisanne was sitting on the porch in one of the wicker chairs their mother had bought years before. She had a blanket wrapped around her and a knit hat on her head. Nights in the desert were always chilly, no matter what time of year.

"A dead-on T-bone," Eve replied. She was on the top step, leaning against the railing. She wore a thick sweater and a scarf. Her knees were pulled up beneath her chin, and she had wrapped her arms around her legs. "I was praying every prayer I knew!" She paused. "And that's a lot of prayers!"

"Man!" Dorisanne had wanted all the details of her sister's near-fatal experience.

The two of them had decided to talk outside while having cups of hot chocolate. The Captain had already gone to bed.

"So Daniel was mad?"

Eve dropped her head, resting her forehead on her knees. "I haven't gotten a talking-to like that since I was thirteen."

Dorisanne took a sip of her hot chocolate. "But you never really said what you were doing out there anyway. Who is this guy again, Russ Biltmore?"

"Ross Biltmore," Eve corrected her. "He's a writer and was a known associate of the murder victim. I was just looking around to see if I could find anything that might shed light on his relationship with the deceased. And I heard some stuff." She made a kind of clicking noise with her tongue. She was happy to have the opportunity to share her ideas with someone.

"I'm pretty sure Biltmore was writing scripts and the victim was getting the credit. There was all this talk between him and Mr. Ewing about money and pages." She shook her head. "At first, I thought it was the producer who had the best motive to commit murder. The two had argued. He thought his director was stealing from him. And I don't know." She hesitated. "There's just something about him I don't like."

"Who?" Dorisanne was clearly interested.

"Ron Polland."

"That's the producer you're talking about?" She seemed impressed. "He's done a lot of famous films," she added. "The Captain said he was working on a Hollywood murder, but I didn't know it was this one. You're trying to solve the case of who killed Charles Cheston?"

Eve smiled. It pleased her that her sister was so excited.

"And who's his client?"

Eve's smile widened.

"You're working for Megan Flint?" Dorisanne practically screamed the question, jumping up and spilling her hot chocolate.

"Shhhhhh!" Eve was worried her sister would wake the Captain.

Dorisanne sat back down. "I can't believe it."

"She's real nice," Eve said. "Sweet, demure. I guess you'd call her beautiful."

"Megan Flint? You've been around her?"

"A lot, actually."

Dorisanne shook her head. "I should have known that if you came home to take care of him, you'd get something big to happen to you like this."

"What's that mean?"

She blew out a breath. She used the blanket to wipe off the spilled cocoa. "It just means I stay with Mama, and the best I get is a male nurse wanting my phone number. You stay with him"—she motioned toward the back of the house—"and you get to meet movie producers and hang out with Hollywood people."

"I don't think that's really the way to look at this," Eve commented.

"Yeah, well, that's true," Dorisanne agreed. "It doesn't matter who shows up. I could never make it through one day of trying to care for him. Mama was a saint."

The two were silent, daughters remembering their mother.

"So, anyway, tell me more about what happened tonight." She drank the last sip of her hot chocolate.

Eve shrugged. Somehow, after hearing the comment that her sister made about caring for their parents, it didn't feel as exciting to share her insights about the murder case.

"Oh, don't do that!" Dorisanne could see what had happened and that Eve had lost interest in the conversation. "Give me some details."

She hesitated a moment. She did want to talk to someone about what she had heard at the cabin.

"Well, now I actually think this Biltmore guy is the better suspect. He had a motive in that he was secretly selling the scripts to Cheston. He left the country when the director disappeared. The victim's car was found near his house." She stopped. "Of course, we don't really have to prove who killed Cheston, we just need to help the attorney come up with a line of defense for Megan that would provide a reasonable doubt that she did it. Offering up another suspect is a way to demonstrate an alternative theory of the crime, but you do have to have evidence to show to the court supporting your claim about another suspect. You don't have to actually prove anything, but you can't just name names and give speculative reports. You have to have a clear theory to present."

There was no response and Eve turned to her sister, who was staring at her. "What?" she asked.

"You sound . . ." Dorisanne paused. "You sound like him." And she pointed to the back of the house.

"Yeah, well, I guess we've been hanging out together a lot the last couple of months."

"Has it been that long?"

Eve nodded. "I know. It's gone by pretty fast."

"Well, it's all very exciting," she noted. "And I'm happy that it's going so well for the two of you."

There was a pause.

"He said his leg was sore." Dorisanne tugged at the blanket that had slipped beneath her shoulders. "That's why he isn't wearing his prosthetic."

Eve considered the lie. She knew the Captain hated anyone to know of a serious medical condition, of a weakness he might have.

She considered holding to his story but then decided Dorisanne had a right to know the truth.

"It got infected," she said, taking a sip from her drink.

"Is it bad?"

Eve shook her head. "I don't think so, no." She put her cup down. "I'm staying for six more weeks," she added.

A look of surprise spread across Dorisanne's face. "Six more weeks?" she asked. "That's a long time to be away from the convent."

Eve shrugged. "I guess." She leaned her head back. "What about the two of you?" She wanted to change the subject. "How did it go after I left?"

Dorisanne closed her eyes. "It was fine," she answered.

Eve watched her sister yawn. She thought about going into the house for the night. It was getting late.

"Did you tell him?" Dorisanne asked, ending the silence.

Eve turned to her sister, who was clearly watching for the answer.

"Tell him what?"

"That I was here before."

Eve glanced away, shaking her head. "No."

"I just couldn't see him, not that night."

"Why? What was going on that night?" Eve recalled it was the first evening they were home from the hospital. She didn't know what was so special about that night to keep her sister away.

"Robbie left me."

"What?" The news was a surprise to Eve. "Why didn't you tell me?"

Dorisanne shrugged. "I didn't want anyone to know."

Eve shook her head. *All these secrets*, she thought. All the ways nobody in her family could tell the truth. She was about to say as much and then thought about herself and the things she knew she had not said to either her sister or the Captain, things like how she wasn't sure she wanted to go back to Pecos, how much she was enjoying trying to help solve a murder.

"Did he come back?"

Dorisanne just shook her head. "I haven't heard from him since that night."

"Could something have happened to him?" She had heard the mention of gambling debts.

"I don't know." She closed her eyes again. "He always seems to hang out with the wrong people."

"Are you safe?" Eve wanted to know.

"I guess," Dorisanne responded.

Eve pulled her feet closer to her, dropping her head onto her knees again. She turned so that she could see her sister's face. The sadness was so obvious, and Eve wondered how she had missed it when Dorisanne had first arrived earlier that evening, how she had not heard it in her voice when they had spoken weeks before. She wondered what else she had missed in her sister's life since moving into the monastery all those years ago.

"I'm sorry, Thumbelina," Eve said, calling her sister by the nickname she had given her when they were just little girls.

Dorisanne didn't answer, but Eve could make out the way her face softened and the slight nod of her head. For all that they had gone through, all that had been shared and missed, Evangeline was sure of one thing—she deeply loved her sister.

FIFTY-EIGHT

"She left a couple of hours ago." The Captain was standing at the kitchen counter. He finished off his coffee, rinsed the cup, and set it in the sink. He spun around on his crutches to face Eve.

"I was going to drive her to the airport." Eve yawned, scratching her head. She was still in her pajamas. "What time is it, anyway?"

"Ten o'clock," he answered. "You were sawing some logs in there, so Dorisanne and I let you sleep."

"You got up to see her off?" She walked over and poured herself a cup of coffee.

He maneuvered his way past her and took a seat at the table. "Isn't that what a father does when his daughter is leaving?"

Eve saw no need to respond. She got out the milk and added some to her drink. She moved over to the table to join him. "What's this?" she asked, reaching for the paper bag in the fruit bowl that served as a centerpiece.

"A burrito from Twila's. I thought you might want some breakfast."

"How did you get to Twila's?" She opened the bag, pulling out the burrito. It was still warm.

"Dorisanne and I drove over there before Michael and Sarah got here to take her to Albuquerque."

Eve nodded. She took a bite. "Yummm." She stopped, bowed her head to say a quick prayer, and kept eating.

"Twila makes the county's best burritos. I don't care what they say over in Albuquerque or Santa Fe." He winked.

"You already eat?"

He nodded.

"You check your sugar level?"

"Yes, and I took my insulin." He reached over to the napkins and handed one to Eve. "And I showered and shaved and even dressed myself."

She rolled her eyes and kept eating.

"Where did you go last night?"

She swallowed hard, took a sip of her coffee, and tried to think of how to respond.

"Never mind," he said. "I already talked to Daniel this morning."

She took another bite.

"He said to tell you that Ewing's story checked out. There was a foal born early this morning, and he also said to tell you that the jet injector is used to vaccinate the horses." He watched her closely. "What's that all about?"

She wiped her mouth. "I saw Daniel last night on the Mine Road."

"When you were on your way to Madeline's?"

She nodded.

"And you talked to John?"

She nodded again.

"And he just happened to have a jet injector in his hand while you had a talk?"

"No, not in his hand."

He waited for an explanation.

She put down the napkin, rested her hands on the table, and decided to tell the truth.

"I went to Mr. Biltmore's house. I saw a jet injector in Mr. Ewing's truck. While I was there, Daniel came up. We were parked at the gate, and Mr. Ewing came flying down the driveway and almost hit us." She took a breath. "We had a short conversation afterward."

He sat back in his chair.

There was a long pause. Eve grabbed the last of her burrito and finished it off.

"Did you find anything out while you were there?"

The question and the interest behind it made Eve smile. She took a sip of her coffee.

"I overheard the two men talking. Cheston definitely was paying Biltmore for the script. He was supposed to come to the house, pick up the script that was left for him, and leave twenty-five thousand dollars in a safe. Biltmore said that the pages he'd left for him were gone, but the money was not there. He said he talked to Cheston the night before he was scheduled to pick up the script."

"Did you hear the date when that call was made?"

She shook her head.

"Did you hear what the script was and where he left it?"

She shook her head again.

"Did you hear anything else?"

"Mr. Ewing drinks whiskey."

The Captain smiled.

She wanted to laugh but showed restraint.

"You know what you did was extremely dangerous, not to mention illegal. And Daniel was pretty sore about tearing his coat jacket, which he refused to give any details about." He eyed Evangeline. "I guess you won't tell me that part of the story."

She shrugged. She figured if Daniel wasn't telling, neither should she.

"Well, it doesn't matter anyway."

She glanced over at him. "What doesn't matter?"

"Any of this," he answered. "Biltmore didn't do it."

"How do you know?"

"Daniel saw him this morning. He admitted he had a business relationship with Cheston. He wrote the scripts and was paid well, and the director took the credit. It had been that way since college. He was happy with the arrangement, never wanted any fame, and he had no beef with Charles."

"Why did he leave the country?" Eve still thought his departure at the time of the victim's disappearance was a little too convenient.

The Captain shook his head. "He goes to India every year about this time. Likes to be at some ashram when the guru shows up. He's got all the receipts to back up his story. He wasn't here. He didn't do it. And if he's telling the truth, with Cheston dead, he loses big."

Eve sat back, pondering these new developments. She was disappointed that Biltmore had been crossed off the suspect list so swiftly. The list was already short, and it was getting shorter by the day.

"That takes us back to either Polland or Cheston's drug dealers." The Captain was thinking the same thing she was. Megan needed the two of them to find a killer.

Eve nodded. She had already talked to Megan about Cheston's suppliers. The young woman was not convinced that the murder had anything to do with her boyfriend's drug habit, and she didn't know where Cheston got the drugs anyway. As far as she knew, Charles had kicked his habit and had no need for a meth source or a dealer of any other illegal substances. But even if he was using, she'd told Eve, she had no idea where the drugs came from. She had never known those details.

"I still think Polland is our best bet," Eve weighed in. "Maybe I should check out this notion he has that Cheston was stealing from him. Maybe if that is the case, that's our best motive for murder."

The Captain nodded. "I called the bank from the back of the calendar you brought home from L.A. Got the name of the person in charge of Cheston's personal finances and found out they do a lot of studio loans and handle a lot of production accounts."

"What's that?"

"A production account is set up for individual film projects. That's where the money comes from for film expenses before and during the production." The Captain pulled out a small notebook he kept in the right front pocket of his shirt. "Elizabeth White is the loan officer in charge of business accounts. Polland Productions is a main customer with various accounts, one of which bears the title 'Project 10: The Way of Broken Trails.'"

Eve smiled. It was certainly the account they would be most interested in.

"And would you like to know who had the authority to withdraw from this account?" He looked up from his pad of paper. He was wearing a big grin.

"I'm guessing Ron Polland," she answered.

"That makes the most sense, yes," he noted. "But usually there are two cosigners on a production account. This allows for a little more accountability in expenditures."

"So, who's the other cosigner?" she wanted to know.

He put the notepad on the table and stretched his arms above his head. "Take another guess," he said, and he waited until Eve was sure she knew the answer.

FIFTY-NINE

Evangeline was in luck. Ron Polland had not left New Mexico and seemed quite happy to meet her somewhere in Santa Fe. He picked the place, some small, out-of-the-way teahouse at the end of Canyon Road. She had dropped the Captain off at Megan's house. He was meeting there with Megan and her attorney to let them know what he had found out about Biltmore and what he felt would be the best defense.

They both liked Lee McDonald, thought he was doing right by Megan, and the Captain was glad to have a chance to meet with him while he was building his case. He had not seen the lawyer since Megan's arraignment, all their communications having been carried out by phone or by e-mail.

Eve pulled into the small parking lot beside the teahouse. She glanced around and saw a black SUV parked in a space nearest the meeting place. She figured it was Polland's car service since there was a driver waiting in the front seat. She made herself a note to check out the license plate before she left. She got out of the truck and walked toward the little shop.

"You made good time." He was waiting for her and held open the door.

"The house you arranged for Megan is very convenient," she said, walking past him. "You must know Santa Fe pretty well."

He pulled the door closed. "I've spent a lot of time here, yes," he responded. "I bought property here before all the other studio shirts even realized New Mexico was a state."

She had to smile. His arrogance entertained her. She knew that Santa Fe had been popular with Californians for more than a few decades. She didn't know how old Polland was, but he certainly did not discover the little town.

They stood at the counter.

"I prefer the white teas," he offered. "They have a beautiful blend from Ethiopia. It has hibiscus."

She thought of her cabdriver in Los Angeles and decided she would have some of the African tea in his honor. Evangeline glanced around the place while he placed their orders. It looked as if the small establishment was at one time a residence, since the room in which they stood opened into other rooms, built like a house, not like a business. She peeked through the door and could see that all the rooms were set up with tables and chairs, the walls covered with art from several continents. There were large pillows in the corners and smaller ones on the seats of the chairs. The window dressings were billowy and attractive. She felt comfortable there and thought the producer had made a nice choice of a meeting location. She liked it.

"Here we go." He handed her a large cup. "There's a table in the back that is a little more private."

She followed him as he walked through the tiny rooms, stopping at the last one. He gestured toward the table in the corner, and she headed over and took a seat. It was by the window, and she took the seat with the view.

"I think you'll like this," he said, taking the other seat. He placed his cup on the table. She did the same.

"Megan seemed okay this morning," she commented, recalling her brief conversation with the young woman when she dropped off the Captain.

"She finally agreed to talk to me," he responded. "Took awhile. And I suppose I owe you an apology as well. I know I came off as a bit boorish."

Eve shrugged. "I probably had it coming," she confessed. She picked up her cup. His hand fell quickly on hers.

"No, wait," he instructed. "You need to let it steep a little longer. The hibiscus takes four minutes to completely release its flavor."

She paused.

"How is your father doing?" he asked, changing the subject.

"He should be able to use the prosthetic again in a few days," she answered.

Polland checked his watch and Eve thought that maybe they needed to move things along, that perhaps he was in a hurry. She was about to ask a question when he touched her on the hand again. "Now," he said, and he took his cup to his lips. He inhaled as if he were smelling a flower, blew on the cup of tea, and took a tiny sip. "Just perfect."

Eve reached for her cup and took a sip. The flavor was so light she wondered if she hadn't waited long enough for the steeping. She lifted her eyebrows. "Nice," she remarked, even though she thought the sturdy black tea they served at the monastery was better than what she was drinking.

"It is a beautiful bouquet of garden flowers."

Eve nodded, taking another sip. She smiled her best fake smile.

"Okay, Sister." He seemed ready to push forward with her agenda. "Why did you call this little meeting? I somehow doubt you have a movie to pitch."

"No," she replied. "No movie." She slid her chair in a bit, moving closer to the table. "I just want to ask you about something you said when I was at the house a couple of days ago."

"Are you asking as a nun or a detective?" he asked.

She didn't answer at first, the question catching her off guard.

"Are you doing private detective work for your father?" he followed up.

She shrugged. "Yes, I am working for my father, so I am asking as a detective." She clasped her hands together.

He grinned.

"You mentioned before that Cheston was stealing from you. Do you have any proof of that?"

He took another small drink of tea. His beverage consumption was a lengthy process.

Eve waited.

"No, I have no proof," he answered. "But I have a very good hunch."

"Where was he stealing the money from?" She wondered

if he would tell her about the bank fund that the Captain had discovered.

"We had a production account. He and I had to cosign to withdraw. I think he managed to take money out without my signature, although I can't prove it."

"Is there money missing from the account?"

He leaned in. "That's what is so interesting," he whispered.

She leaned in as well.

"I couldn't check the balance for a week, password was changed for some reason. Then, right after Cheston was murdered, I got into the account, pronto."

She waited, expecting to hear that twenty-five thousand dollars was missing, the amount owed to Biltmore. She guessed that if the victim needed money, it was to pay the writer. Since she had heard the amount that was owed to Biltmore, she figured this would be the amount missing from the production account.

"It was all there." His body snapped back.

She shook her head. "All of it?"

"Every penny," he said. And he swallowed another bit of tea.

Eve did the same.

"When I called the bank and talked to Betsy, I asked about the week I couldn't get into the account, and she just said it was some bank error and that it had been rectified." He lifted his shoulders slightly and said, "I'll probably never know what really happened."

"Wait." There was something he'd said that had caught her attention. "There's someone at the bank named Betsy?"

"Betsy White," he answered. "She's an assistant manager of the accounts. Nice girl. Wants to be an actress."

"Elizabeth White is Betsy White?" she asked, recalling the name the Captain had reported as the bank representative.

"I guess so. I don't know."

"I've heard that name somewhere."

"You're probably thinking of Betty White. She's a Hollywood legend."

"No, it's not Betty. It's Betsy. Where did I hear that?" And suddenly she remembered.

SIXTY

——— ✦❖✦ ———

"I don't know, Evangeline."

She had used Polland's cell phone to call the Captain.

"It sounds like a stretch to me."

"Well, just ask her." She wanted to find out more about the woman named Betsy who Megan had mentioned. "She told me that Betsy was the name of somebody who had been promised a part in Cheston's movie. She had heard a phone message from Betsy intended for the victim. She called her back. Ask Megan for the number. Just find out if it's the woman at the bank."

"Okay, okay." There was a pause. "You still with Polland?"

She looked across the table at the empty seat. "He's getting us another cup of tea."

"He tell you anything?"

"Just that he thinks Cheston took the money from that production account and that he wasn't able to access it for a few days. Then, after the murder, he was able to get into the account and check the balance."

"And?"

"And it was all there."

She could hear the sigh. "That doesn't really give us anything to go on."

"Just ask Megan about this woman she called, and I'll see you in a little while."

Polland walked back into the room. He squeezed her on the shoulder and she flinched. He pulled away, getting the message loud and clear.

She handed him the small phone. "I don't know how to turn it off," she said.

He pressed a button, put the phone in his pocket, and sat down. "Your father agree with you?"

She assumed he meant her idea about the bank manager. "He said he'd talk to Megan, get some more information."

"That's not what I asked."

"I'm not sure I understand the question."

"Does your father agree that I'm a viable suspect?"

She picked up the cup of tea he had set on the table before her. She glanced up and then put it back down. She knew to wait. "I think he's open to the possibility."

He nodded.

"You do have a motive," she suggested.

"And that is?"

"Cheston wasn't delivering the work you wanted. He had let you down. You were fed up with his drug habit. And according to you, he was stealing from you." She stopped. "And there could be something else," she added.

He tilted his head in her direction. "I'm all ears," he said.

"Maybe you want Megan. Maybe you love her."

He locked eyes with Eve, sat back, and took a sip from his second cup of tea. "What would you know about love, Sister?"

"Not very much, I imagine. But I know enough."

He took another sip, savoring it.

"What about you?" she asked, turning the tables. "You seem to know a lot about those of us choosing the religious life. You seem to know all our dirty, little secrets. You said the priesthood wasn't a good fit for you." She drank some tea. "I'm guessing it was the vow of celibacy that did it for you. Although I'm sure the idea of poverty wasn't all that attractive for you either."

He didn't respond, appearing to ignore the dig.

"But maybe it wasn't sleeping around you were interested in. Maybe you wanted what a lot of people want."

"And that is?"

"Maybe you wanted to settle down, have a wife and kids." She paused, expecting him to jump in with another comeback.

He didn't.

She kept going. "Only, I don't see a ring on your finger. I never hear you talk about a family. So it makes me wonder, is Megan the one?"

He put down his cup, breathed a long breath, and placed his hands in his lap. *It was all very dramatic*, Eve thought.

"No," he answered solemnly. "Megan is not the one. Unlike most of my colleagues, I know better than to mix business with pleasure. Megan has a contract with me."

Eve didn't respond.

He continued. "I snatched her up from Podunk, Kansas, or wherever she's from, and made her a star. She owes me, and we're both comfortable with that arrangement. She's more like my daughter than my lover."

Eve nodded. She wasn't sure she believed him, but it was making an interesting story. "I may not know much about love, as you so clearly pointed out, but I do know that loyalty is intrinsic to all intimate relationships. Husband and wife, parent and child. Maybe you hated what Cheston was doing to Megan and you wanted to put a stop to it. Maybe she feels like a daughter you wanted to protect."

"Is that what your father would do?"

The question came as a complete surprise.

SIXTY-ONE

Another couple entered the room and sat at the table opposite theirs. They chatted about some piece of art they had just admired at one of the galleries down the street.

Polland was still waiting for her answer.

"Yes," she answered, thinking about the Captain. "He would want to put a stop to anything that he thought was hurting me or my sister."

"Even if it meant killing a man?"

Eve pondered the question. Would the Captain commit murder if he thought the man was a threat to herself or to Dorisanne?

She took another sip of her tea and remembered overhearing a private conversation that was held right after her sister's wedding. She had needed something from her bedroom, and she had left the wedding party being held outside at her parents' home and gone inside the house to get it. A jacket, her camera, she didn't remember. When she stepped into the hallway, she heard a tense exchange. The voices were familiar. Two men: Robbie, her new brother-in-law; and the Captain.

"How much do you owe them?" she'd heard the Captain ask.

There was a muttered response followed by silence. She thought she heard a paper rip. *From a checkbook?* she had wondered.

"I'll give you this as a wedding present, and I won't ask for anything in return. But I'm telling you right now, Robert." Eve recalled being surprised at hearing that name. She had never realized Robbie was short for Robert. "If you bring my daughter down, if you hurt her in any way, and I don't just mean physically, I mean if you break her heart or ruin her dreams or her reputation, if you do anything to sully her name, I'll find you, son. I'll hunt you down and make you burn."

Eve recalled how she suddenly couldn't breathe, the words she was hearing were so harsh, so stern.

"Am I making myself clear?" he had asked, the way he always asked when he'd cornered someone or wanted some confirmation that he was understood.

And again there had been only a mumbled response. And that had been it. Eve had quickly left the hallway and gone back to the party.

Accompanying the memory, Eve also had the notion that Dorisanne may have lost contact with her husband in recent weeks because he remembered this conversation too. Maybe Robbie wasn't running from Dorisanne, maybe he was running from the Captain.

She turned to the producer. "To answer your question, there's no doubt about it," she said. "He could do it easily."

She could see that Polland understood what she was saying,

but she decided to go ahead and finish the thought anyway. "He would kill a man in a heartbeat if he thought his daughter had been harmed."

"Then I'd say you're lucky to have a dad like that," he responded and stood up to take his leave.

Eve stood as well.

"But to answer your question about Megan and me, no, I am not her jealous lover or her overprotective father figure. I care about her, but I wouldn't kill for her."

Evangeline watched as he quickly finished his last bit of tea.

He turned and headed for the door. "You coming?" he asked.

She nodded and joined him, thinking about what had just transpired between them. She was surprised at how much her world was expanding. She thought she knew everything there was to know about her family, about her relationship with the Captain. More and more she was discovering she didn't really know that much at all.

SIXTY-TWO

———— ⟨✳⟩⟨✳⟩ ————

"You want me to take another trip to Los Angeles?" Evangeline was driving back to Madrid. She was excited about the news she was only just hearing, news that Betsy White was in fact the woman Megan had called and the manager of the production account at the bank. And she was happy to make another jaunt to the West Coast.

"I don't think we need you to confront Ms. White," the Captain answered. "Let's let the attorney and the L.A. police handle it from this point on." He pulled on the strap of his seat belt.

Even though he didn't want to admit it, Eve thought he acted a little excited as well.

"So, you talked to her?" She knew the Captain had made the call to the bank once it was confirmed that the number Megan still had in her recent calls list on her cell phone matched the contact number for Elizabeth White shown on the bank website.

"First I talked to her supervisor," he answered, "then I talked to her."

"Well . . ." She waited, turning to look at her passenger. "What did they say?"

Eve had wanted details when she arrived at Megan's house, but the Captain hadn't allowed a conversation. Every time she would ask a question, he would block it with some other topic. Only later when they both got in the truck did he explain that he didn't think it best to talk about this new development in front of his client.

"Better to have a little more to report," he had said.

"Tell me," she pleaded.

He released the strap. "The supervisor confirmed that Elizabeth White, known to her friends as Betsy, handled all Polland Productions accounts. She was therefore in charge of the one labeled 'Project 10: The Way of Broken Trails,' which required signatures from both Mr. Polland and Mr. Cheston to make withdrawals."

Eve clapped her hands on the steering wheel. "This is it!" she shouted.

"Hold on there, Sister," the Captain responded. "We don't have nearly enough to go to the police yet."

"What about Betsy? What did she have to say?"

He smiled. "Ms. White was hesitant to tell me much about the account or about her relationship with Mr. Polland or Mr. Cheston. She confirmed being the account representative and knowing both men. She also said that she was deeply saddened about the death of her client and that Mr. Polland had changed the details of the account, removing Cheston's name from the required signature list and adding Mr. Leon Joiner, the chief financial officer of the production company." He paused. "That's standard when there has been a death."

Eve nodded. "Did you ask her if she had spoken to Megan?"

"She denied that," he answered. "And she denies that she and the victim ever talked about her having an acting role in his picture."

Eve sped up and took the highway exit a bit faster than anticipated.

"You trying to kill us?" The Captain had braced himself to keep from sliding across the seat.

"Sorry," she said, taking her foot off the gas pedal. The truck slowed.

"Thank you," he noted.

"Was there anything else from the conversation that helps us?" she wanted to know.

He glanced over at Evangeline. "Well, if you must know, her supervisor claims Ms. White has been taking acting lessons. He had even been to see her in a local play of some kind. When I asked him if she had aspirations to be a star, he laughed and said, 'Doesn't every girl in Hollywood?' He thought he was pretty funny."

"So she lied." Evangeline thought this was good news. "The account manager did want a role in Cheston's film."

"Looks that way," he replied.

"Well, that wouldn't be hard to prove, right?"

"That she lied or that she wants to be an actress?"

She thought about the question. "Either one. If she wants to be an actress, she lied about not being interested in a movie role." She clapped her hands on the wheel again. "We've got her! All we have to do is get a search warrant, and I bet we'll find all the evidence we need."

There was no response.

"What's wrong?" She could see the cloud that had moved across his face.

He shook his head. "It's not going to be that easy to get a search warrant. It's going to take a lot for the police or the district attorney to be interested enough to check out this woman. It's like I told you awhile back, if a detective has a suspect and starts moving down that path, he doesn't like to be told to take another one."

"Even if he's wrong?"

"Especially if he's wrong."

She shook her head. "I don't understand."

He faced her but did not respond.

"You don't look for somebody else," he said.

"What do you mean?" She wouldn't accept his answer. "Even if there is evidence or a really strong lead, a police officer wouldn't check it out? Before a conviction is handed down, wouldn't an officer want to make sure they had the right person? Wouldn't they want to look at every possibility?"

He rested his elbow on the door. "In their minds, every other possibility has been eliminated. They've already narrowed down the list of potential perpetrators. They picked Megan Flint. Nobody wants to back off from their number one suspect. Nobody wants to admit they were wrong."

"So the entire police force would just squelch Megan's attorney's request to check out this other lead? Even one as solid as Betsy White at the bank?"

"I'm afraid so, Eve."

She blew out a long breath and kept shaking her head.

"It just happens," he added. "You get in this pattern of police investigations, and you don't want to believe you can make a mistake. You don't want to think you charged the wrong person, believed the wrong story. If you start to doubt yourself, you quit being an effective officer of the law."

Eve turned to look at the Captain. "Is that what happened to you?"

Something about the way he was describing this situation sounded very personal. He looked away, pulled down the visor, and rested his head against the back of his seat. "I made a big mistake," he confessed. "I arrested the wrong guy, kept him in jail for two years." His voice had softened. "Kept him away from his family, his job, everything, because I was so sure that I was right and he had committed the crime."

Eve watched the road, keeping both hands on the steering wheel.

"But I was wrong. And by the time the evidence was released that proved I was wrong, this guy had lost everything." He cleared his throat.

Eve didn't look, but she knew the emotion had overcome him and made him stop. She heard him take a breath.

"He got out of jail, went to his house that had been taken over by the bank, called his wife who had moved away and divorced him to tell her he loved her and to say good-bye to his little girl, and then he got a gun and shot himself."

Eve kept driving.

"I put in for my retirement the next day." He reached up, turned the handle, and rolled down the window.

A cool breeze filled the cab of the truck, and the outside noise kept there from being any further conversation.

SIXTY-THREE

"What if Polland talks to her?" Eve asked.

Evangeline and the Captain had driven back to Santa Fe the day after the calls were made to the bank where Elizabeth White worked. Lee McDonald tried everything he could to get the police chief or the district attorney to check out the motive and the bank manager's story, but they would have nothing to do with it.

"What if he talks to her like he trusts her or maybe like he has a part for her in the movie after all? He could use a tape recorder or something. Maybe she'd confess everything to him."

It was late in the evening and they were home, sitting on the front porch. Trooper rested between them.

"It's actually amazing to me how much people will tell you. I used to think people were confessing to me all the time because of the habit, because they could tell I was a nun and they immediately assumed it was what they should do. But even without the habit and veil, if you ask the right questions or even act like you're interested, people will tell you anything."

"People just don't talk to everybody," the Captain responded.

"No?" Eve asked.

"No," he answered.

"Hmm." The news surprised her.

"You've always had that gift," he added.

"A gift?"

"People wanting to talk to you, tell you things." He turned to her. "You know this, right?"

Eve shrugged. "I just thought that's what people did."

He shook his head. "No, Evangeline, people don't tell things to just anybody and everybody. They have to feel like they trust you."

She didn't respond.

"Guess that's what makes you a good nun." He reached over and gave Trooper a welcomed scratch behind her ears. "And a good PI."

The compliment was unexpected. Eve was at a loss for words. She cleared her throat and then all she could do was acknowledge what had been said with a nod. She had never felt so validated or appreciated in her life. She wanted the moment to last.

"He can use his phone," the Captain responded, breaking the silence.

"What?"

"His phone—he doesn't need a tape recorder. He can record a conversation with his cell phone."

Eve shook her head. "There are so many things I don't know," she said. "A phone that records conversations—I have to get one of those things."

"You think you'll need one at the convent?" the Captain asked.

He was fishing, she could tell.

"So, if we can get him in there with her . . ." She was ignoring the comment. "He could just keep his phone close by and record what she says."

The Captain nodded.

"You think he can act?"

"From what I've seen, everybody in that business thinks they can act."

Eve smiled and leaned over, nudging the Captain in the side. He grabbed her by the arm and held it for just a second. Then he let go, giving her a few pats when he did.

It was the only show of affection she had received from him since her mother died. She waited and then pulled away.

"All right, let's see what the talented Mr. Polland can do," she said, summing up the conversation and feeling her heart swell.

SIXTY-FOUR

---※※---

"I know you don't want to confess to anything, and I don't blame you for that, but just tell me how it happened, Betsy, tell me how you got to Cheston, and just know that I am a huge fan. I am so glad he's gone."

There was a giggle.

"Just let me in on some of the details of how it happened, how you found him, how you killed him, because I think in addition to acting, you may have a future in writing scripts. I just know this one is ready for prime time, baby."

Evangeline turned to the Captain and rolled her eyes. The two of them had gathered at his office with Megan to listen to the recording Polland had sent them via e-mail. The producer had made the trip to Los Angeles, scheduled a meeting at his office with Elizabeth White, and after a couple of glasses of wine, she'd made a complete confession. He recorded the entire conversation between the two of them.

"Well . . ." A small feminine voice began to take over the recording. "He came to me not long after you opened up the account and offered to take me on a studio tour after work one day. We had drinks and dinner a couple of times after that. Then a couple of weeks later, he came to the bank and said he was going to New Mexico to tie up some loose ends for this project, that he had to make arrangements for a final location, and that he needed some extra cash to take with him. When I explained that he couldn't make a withdrawal without both signatures, that's when he mentioned that he had been thinking about something ever since he met me that first day at the bank. He said that especially after spending a little time with me, he was certain that I was perfect for the lead in the film."

"And I absolutely agree with him. You are perfect."

"I knew letting him have the money was wrong, Mr. Polland."

"Yes, yes, I know. Cheston could be so charming when he wanted something."

Evangeline looked at Megan. The young woman had dropped her eyes and was staring at the table in front of her.

"He could, couldn't he? Anyway, he promised me that he would get the money back in the account in less than a week, and that I just needed to give him the withdrawal, keep the slip for a few days, and find a way to not let you access the account."

"You changed the password," Polland said.

There was no verbal response, but it was easy to figure out that she was nodding at this point in the conversation. "But I changed it back, you saw that, right?"

"I did," he answered.

"And the money is there."

"Yes, it is all there, and I thank you for that."

There was another giggle.

"But, Elizabeth, what made you want to kill him?"

"He lied. I found out from his girlfriend that there was no part for me and certainly not the lead. She made it very clear that she had that role." There was a break. "Is that water? Can I have some water?"

"Of course." And there was the sound of something being poured into a glass. "Here you go."

"Thanks."

Another break.

"So, you flew to New Mexico to confront him?"

"No, I drove."

"My goodness, Betsy, that's a long trip."

"Twenty hours there and back, but it took even longer because I hadn't expected his girlfriend to be there."

"Megan."

"They were fighting. He told me when we had dinner here in L.A. that he was breaking up with her, that he had divorced his wife and Megan was just a rebound experience. He said he never loved her and that she was having a hard time accepting the fact that he was breaking up with her. She was so needy. She claimed she had to have the work to pay for her mother in an institution. She's crazy." There was another giggle. "He said she was intolerable. That's how he said it, needy and intolerable."

Evangeline turned again to Megan. They locked eyes and Megan's began to fill with tears.

The Captain saw the reaction. He hit the Stop button on the computer screen. The conversation halted. "We don't have to listen to this right now." He watched Megan.

Eve reached over and took the young woman by the hand. "He's right," she added. "We can listen to it and then tell you what was said, tell you how it happened."

She shook her head and wiped her face with a tissue. "No, I'm fine. I want to hear it."

He hesitated and then switched the recording back on.

SIXTY-FIVE

⸻ ✤ ⸻

"So, I just watched the house until he left real early in the morning. I followed him to a cabin off a dirt road."

"A cabin?"

Evangeline glanced over at the Captain. They both realized that Polland didn't know about any of this. In this part of the conversation he wasn't acting. He didn't know about Biltmore and the scripts being written by someone else.

"Way out somewhere. He was picking up the last pages of the script for this movie." There was a pause. "I have them if you want them."

"Of course," he answered. "And Cheston was picking them up at this cabin?"

It sounded as if she was taking a drink.

"And that's when you killed him?"

There was a gasp. "I didn't mean to kill him," she said.

"I'm sure you didn't. He probably got physical with you, and you just did it out of self-defense."

Everything was quiet for a moment.

"No, it wasn't that."

"Oh?"

"I just meant to scare him. I had a dart gun. I got it from a friend who works for the state parks department, wildlife and game division. He's the one they call when they need to tranquilize a mountain lion or bear. He's starting his own business, wants to work as an animal wrangler for the movie studios."

"Did your friend know you had his dart gun?"

The Captain smiled. He jotted down a note and passed it to Evangeline.

You were right! Handles himself pretty well in an interview, he had written.

Eve nodded.

"No. I took it when I went out to his place to drop off his loan papers. That's how we met," she explained. "I was helping him with his business loan."

"So, you stole this dart gun and the tranquilizer, shot him, and it killed him."

There was a soft whimper. "I didn't mean to kill him. I didn't mean to kill anybody."

"There, there, Betsy, of course you didn't. It's okay. It's just fine."

More weeping.

"I didn't know what to do, so I just dragged him into my SUV and started driving. When I realized he was dead, I was so upset. I just drove and drove, and I ended up in another little town and out past this horse-stables place, and I just stopped and rolled him out of the car." She blew her nose. "I guess it snowed later and that's why it took a few days to find him."

"I think that's right. I think there was a lot of snow."

"I guess I was lucky about that."

"Yes, I guess you were."

There was a pause.

"So then what happened?"

"Then I just went back to where his car was, drove it up the road a ways until I could hide it really well, and then I walked back to the cabin where my car was and I drove home. I took his laptop and his cell phone and those script pages and I just came home."

"That's some story, Betsy."

"You really don't think I'm a bad person for killing Mr. Cheston?"

"I do not."

"And do you really think I could be the lead in your movie?"

"I think you have already proven that you have some undeniable skills."

The Captain reached over and stopped the recording.

"What happens now?" Evangeline asked.

"Now, we hope that the police and the DA have already listened to their copies of this recording and that they have found Ms. Elizabeth White and taken her in for questioning. And that Mr. McDonald is standing in front of some judge explaining why all of the charges need to be dropped against his client."

"They can't really use this as a confession, can they?" Eve wanted to know.

"Well, not in court, but certainly to persuade Ms. White to tell the story one more time to them."

Evangeline glanced over at Megan, who still had her head down and had not spoken a word since the recording stopped.

"You okay, Meg?"

She nodded. "Sounded like a scene out of a movie," she said.

"It did," Evangeline responded.

"Maybe Ron will make it and I'll get a good part. Maybe I could play myself. Maybe I could finally win an Oscar."

Eve watched the young woman as she tried to gather herself. She smoothed down the sides of her hair and blotted her face with the tissue. And then she took in a deep breath, dropping her hands in her lap.

"Megan, I'm sure it might be your most challenging role, but with or without awards and recognition, being true to yourself will never let you down." Eve glanced over at the young woman, who smiled sadly, and when she turned back to the Captain, he was watching her closely.

SIXTY-SIX

"That's it then?" Evangeline watched as the Captain walked out of the room, trying out his prosthetic once again. "This will stop his pain and get him back to normal?"

"That's it," Ricky replied from the floor where he still sat on his knees after adjusting the artificial limb. "I added a small strip of lamb's wool to the top strap. That should keep it from rubbing against his leg." He reached around and picked up the box and the bits of trash that he had left on the floor. "He and Peggy should be good to go." He laughed. "That still cracks me up."

"Yeah, he is one funny guy."

"Ricky!" the Captain shouted from the kitchen. "Let's take a walk."

"Coming, Mr. Divine."

"It's *Diveen*."

"What?" He had stood up and was getting ready to walk out of the room.

"The last name. It's not Divine, it's *Diveen*."

"Are you sure?"

Evangeline just stared at the young man. "It's my name," she said, trying to refrain from the sarcasm.

"That's crazy," he replied. "I keep wanting to say Divine, like, you know, heavenly or something."

"I know," she said. "You're not the only one. I've heard that all my life."

"That's so cool." He had the box and bag of trash under his arm. "Maybe you should be a nun or something."

"Maybe," she said, offering no explanation. Clearly, no one had told the young man about her vocation.

"Or maybe you are a nun, but it's a secret identity. Like one of those superheroes who look all normal during the day but at night become . . . *secretly divine*." Ricky walked past her. He laughed.

Evangeline nodded. "Right," she said. "Maybe that's it."

She glanced around the room at the Captain's personal belongings. Except for a bit more clutter and a little more dust, the bedroom had not changed since her mother died three years before. He kept her jewelry box on the dresser, her lace doilies on the nightstand; the pictures she had selected remained on the wall. Eve knew her clothes were still folded in the drawers and hanging in the closet. It was like he was still waiting for her to come home.

She sat on the bed. Her mother died in this bedroom, arranged her good-byes, and took her final breath surrounded by all three of her family members. A couple of days before she died, she called for Eve and Dorisanne. It had been a struggle for her to talk at that point, but she had things she needed to say.

"I know you don't always get along with your father. But he's not what you think," she had said. "He loves you. He doesn't always know how to show you, but he does."

"Mama, I don't want to talk about him right now," Eve had replied.

"We need to talk about this, Eve. All of us need to talk about this."

She struggled to breathe.

"We've had so many good times together, the three of us. We've laughed so much and enjoyed so many things. He's always felt like he was on the outside, you know. He never knew how to be with three women, and we never really made it all that easy for him. So, just try, okay?" She had reached up and taken both of her daughters by the hand. "Just try to let him in, a little, okay?"

And the two daughters had made the promise to their dying mother.

SIXTY-SEVEN

---※※---

"You coming?" He was standing at the door. "Ricky and I thought you were walking with us. We're going up the road a bit."

Eve cleared her throat and wiped her eyes. She was sitting on his bed.

"What's wrong with you?" He came a little closer. "Are you all right?"

She nodded. "I was just thinking about Mama," she answered.

He stood beside her and then nudged her arm. She moved over and he sat down.

"I miss her," Eve said, the words choking in her throat.

"Yeah, me too," he agreed. "I'm not much good without her," he confessed. "She always was the best thing I had going for me."

Eve nodded again. She was finding it difficult to talk.

"She loved you girls, that's for sure." He reached over and patted her on the leg. "And both of you look like her." He shook his head. "Dorisanne with her dancer's body, you with her dark eyes, dark brown hair. Sometimes it's hard for me to even look at the two of you because all I see is her."

Eve laughed a bit.

"Oh, Sam Hill, I guess that didn't come out right." He moved his hand over and rubbed the top of his thigh. "I do that a lot with the two of you for some reason. It's like I don't know how to talk to either one of you. Like I never really learned how because she always did it for me."

"You do okay," Eve finally responded.

He nodded, receiving the affirmation. "Look, I don't know what's going on with you and the convent. I figure you're old enough to know what you want, but . . ." He paused.

She turned to face him, uncertain of what he was trying to say. "But what?"

"But I just need to tell you that if you want to stay here a little longer, I'm happy to ask your boss to give you a few more weeks. I don't mind telling him I need your help around here. I don't mind telling him that at all."

Eve smiled. She took him by the hand. "No, I've done that long enough." She took in a breath. "I'm sorry I used what was going on with you to run from the truth. I need to talk to my superiors about what has happened. I need to tell the truth. I'm going to talk to them about everything."

He nodded and was about to stand up.

"But I need to tell you something else."

He sat back down.

"These three months that we have been together have been important to me, really, the best three months I've had in a long time."

He smiled. "You're a fine investigator, Evangeline. I always knew you would be."

"You did, didn't you?"

He reached across her and gave her a squeeze. "But you're a fine nun, too, and I'm sure your superior will tell you the same thing. So, I guess you're going to have to make up your mind about what you want to do. You have to figure out what's going to make you happy. And I'll support you in whatever you want to do."

She nodded, her eyes filling up again.

"Yo, Mr. Divine, you coming or what? I need to see if Peggy's going to hold." Ricky was calling from somewhere in the front of the house.

"I keep telling him it's *Diveen*," she said. "He doesn't seem to listen."

"Aw, he's just a kid," he replied. "He can't shake the idea of wanting to be close to something great, that he's searching for anything better or more than what he knows he'll find in this world." He yanked at his pants legs, pulling them down. "Shoot, saying it that way, I guess we're all hoping for the divine."

Eve smiled. "Yeah, Dad, I guess that's true."

The two stood together and headed up the hallway. She stopped as they got to the front door.

He turned to her. "You coming?"

She shook her head. "No, I have to make a call," she answered. "You go ahead. We'll walk again later."

He nodded, opened the door, and walked outside. Eve headed over to the phone in the kitchen. It was time she said the things that needed to be said.

EPILOGUE

Evangeline sat in the dark theater as the credits rolled. There it was: Charles Cheston's name. Following the list of songs available on the sound track, a full-screen acknowledgment read "In memory of Charles Cheston. Thank you for finding the best stories and the most wonderful locations."

Evangeline thought it was tasteful and not too over the top, simple and honest. She had never met the famed director but figured he would have wanted more.

The Way of Broken Trails turned out to be only a moderate success as far as big-budget films went, but for all the people of Madrid the movie and its production were a win. The entire project was shot on location, and for months the Madrid businesses flourished as they never had before. Megan Flint, the female lead of the science-fiction, Western movie, bought the property where she and Cheston had stayed on their prior visits. Ross Biltmore became the credited scriptwriter, and Polland turned in a very

surprising and well-received performance as the movie's director
and producer.

The leading man was some big name that Eve didn't recognize
but one that Dorisanne and Daniel thought had been perfect in
the role. They both knew everything there was to know about the
star, including his bio and favorite meal, the steak and green chile
breakfast burrito at Twila's. Dorisanne had come back to Madrid
for a few weeks to watch the filming, and Daniel had been in
charge of security on the set.

The four of them, along with Jackson's prosthetist, Ricky, traveled
together by limousine to the all-star premiere that was held at the
Lensic, Santa Fe's most renowned theater. Eve and the Captain were
reunited with Megan for the first time since the case had been closed
and she had left New Mexico to head back to California. Before the
movie began, the young star asked for the microphone and tearfully
introduced both father and daughter as her private detective team.
She credited the two with saving her life and pointing her in the right
direction, and she happily announced that her next project was the
film based on her breakout memoir, *The Best Role I'll Ever Play*.

The evening had been a lovely occasion for the Divine family
and their friends, and afterward everyone gathered at the Mineshaft
in Madrid for a party. There was live music from Bill and Bonnie
Hearne, favorite local musicians, green chile stew, freshly made
tamales, posole, and more than a few kegs of beer. Later, it would
go down as the liveliest and longest town celebration ever, since
singing was still emanating from the bar when Eve walked past
the Mineshaft on her way to the office the following day. She had
taken the long hike from her father's house into town.

She laughed when she heard Marcie trying to run out the final stragglers. "Go home, you two!" she heard the owner shout. "I got to clean this place up so I can open in an hour. I got a lunch shift, you know, and those tourists need their burgers and beer!"

Evangeline walked past the bar and stood at the door to her father's office. The sign that read "Divine Private Detective Agency" had started to lean a little to the left. She walked over and straightened it, dusted it off, and then stepped back to admire her work.

"That was quite a party."

She turned around. Dorisanne was wearing running shoes and a sweat suit. Eve figured her sister must have left the house not too long after she had.

"I'm surprised you're up," Eve replied.

"I heard you leave," Dorisanne said. "I thought you were just going out for the paper. When you didn't come back right away, I got dressed and tried to catch up with you, but you had already gotten past the hill."

Eve smiled at her sister. They'd been enjoying their time together. She had promised to drive her to the airport later for her flight back to Las Vegas. Dorisanne was excited because she had an audition later that week for a new show being produced by one of Polland's good friends. She was a shoo-in for a part as a dancer.

"You working here now?"

Evangeline turned again and faced the door of their father's business. She shrugged. "I've been back at the monastery for almost nine months now."

"I know," Dorisanne replied. "I was here when you finished your leave and went back, remember?"

Eve turned around. "Mr. Salazar hired Daddy to find some gold he thinks is buried on his property."

"Hmm."

"Twila wants him to find her sister."

Dorisanne raised her eyebrows. "Twila has a lost sister?"

Eve nodded. "Guess so."

They both turned to watch a car pulling into the parking lot beside the Mineshaft. A family of four exited the vehicle, talking and laughing.

"You didn't answer my question."

"I took another leave of absence," Eve finally responded. "For myself this time, for me to try and figure things out. So, yes, while I'm here, I'm going to help out in the office."

Daisy rounded the corner and Eve bent down to give the animal a good scratch.

"They still making the nuns move out of the monastery, separate the men from the women?"

Eve nodded. "Most of the other sisters are staying, a couple have left."

"Are they going to build a kennel?"

Eve shook her head. She had told her sister about the building project and her hopes of getting the plans changed to include a small kennel for the stray animals she kept housing. She stood up.

"You can build one back here," Dorisanne suggested.

Eve glanced around the office, down the street at Firehouse Lane. She had never actually thought about that possibility. *It could happen*, she thought.

There was a pause.

"I guess he's glad you're hanging around."

She nodded. "Seems to be."

Dorisanne glanced over in the direction of the sign her sister had just straightened. She acted as if she were studying it. "Maybe you should change the name," she said.

Eve looked at the office sign and guessed that Dorisanne was referring to the common mispronunciation of their last name. She figured her sister was talking about the plan they had made when they were young, to change the spelling from Divine to Diveen.

"Private Detectives," Dorisanne said, not intending a change to the last name at all. "Just get rid of the word 'agency' and call it Divine Private Detectives. Make it plural."

"Oh." Eve smiled. "That." She shrugged. "Well, I'm not quite sure it's time to make that kind of a change. My leave is only for a few weeks."

"Okay," Dorisanne said. "It's your life."

"Yes," she answered. "As unsure as I am about what to do with it, that much is true." And she opened the door and stood aside, inviting her sister in.

READING GROUP GUIDE

1. Sister Evangeline struggles between her vocation as a nun and her passion for solving mysteries. What do you think were her reasons for becoming a nun? What are her reasons for considering leaving the order?

2. What gifts does Evangeline have that make her a good detective?

3. Megan strikes a chord in Eve, draws her to the case. What about Megan pulls Eve into the work of being a detective?

4. What role does Mother Madeline play in Evangeline's life?

5. How does the father-daughter relationship of the Captain and Eve evolve in this story? Is it better in the end that it was in the beginning?

6. Divine is pronounced Diveen; Madrid is not pronounced like the city in Spain—what else is not what it appears in this story?

7. How does visiting her mother's grave help Eve know how to best support the Captain? What is the memory that gives her answers?

8. Why do both daughters seem to have such difficulty with their father?

9. What has Evangeline missed in the life of her family by being in the convent?

10. Do you think Evangeline will go back to the convent at the end of the leave of absence?

ACKNOWLEDGMENTS

I am grateful to the kind folks at HCCP, especially publisher, Daisy Hutton, my lovely and sharp-eyed editor, Ami McConnell, and the other members of that talented staff, including Ansley Boatman, Karli Cajka, Amanda Bostic, and Deborah Wiseman. Also thanks to the hardworking women who handled all of the marketing and publicity: Kerri Potts and Laura Dickerson. I am honored to be a part of such a strong and devoted team as the fiction division at the HarperCollins Christian Publishing Group. Thank you for your many kindnesses extended to me and for embracing the stories of Sister Eve!

ALSO BY LYNNE HINTON

FICTION
Friendship Cake
Hope Springs
Forever Friends
Christmas Cake
Wedding Cake
The Things I Know Best
The Last Odd Day
The Arms of God
The Order of Things
Pie Town
Welcome Back to Pie Town

WRITING UNDER THE NAME LYNNE BRANARD
The Art of Arranging Flowers

WRITING UNDER THE NAME JACKIE LYNN
Down by the Riverside
Jacob's Ladder
Swing Low, Sweet Chariot

NONFICTION
Meditations for Walking

ABOUT THE AUTHOR

Lynne Hinton is the New York Times bestselling author of *Friendship Cake* and *The Art of Arranging Flowers*, along with 16 other books. She holds a Masters of Divinity degree from Pacific School of Religion in Berkeley, California. She has served as hospice chaplain, church pastor, and retreat leader. Lynne is a regular columnist with *The Charlotte Observer*. A native of North Carolina, She lives with her husband and dog in Albuquerque, New Mexico. Visit Lynne's website at www.lynnehinton.com and Facebook: Lynne-Hinton-Books.